MAKING SENSE OF
PAUL

MAKING SENSE OF
PAUL

*A Basic Introduction to
Pauline Theology*

VIRGINIA WILES

HENDRICKSON PUBLISHERS

Hendrickson Publishers, Inc.
P.O. Box 3473
Peabody, Massachusetts 01961-3473

Printed in the United States of America

First printing — February 2000

Except where otherwise noted, Scripture quotations are from the New Revised Standard Version of the Bible copyright © 1989 by the Division of Christian Education of the National Council of the Churches of Christ in the United States of America and are used by permission.

Library of Congress Cataloging-in-Publication Data

Wiles, Virginia, 1954–
    Making sense of Paul : a basic introduction to Pauline theology / Virginia Wiles.
        p. cm.
    Includes bibliographical references.
    ISBN 1-56563-117-X (pbk.)
    1. Bible. N.T. Epistles of Paul—Theology. 2. Paul, the Apostle, Saint. I. Title.

BS2651 .W48 2000
225.9′2—dc21

99-098001

For Ginny and Jaclyn

Table of Contents

Part Three: Paul's Creative Contribution

List of Illustrations

Preface

I first began this volume as a concentrated effort to articulate the theology of Paul for undergraduate students who had neither background in Paul nor initial interest in theology. As the writing has progressed, I have made the manuscript available not only to my students but also to numerous adult laypeople and seminary students. The positive response of these interested adults to what was initially written for college-age students has surprised and delighted me, and thus has affected the final version of the volume. Although the imprint of my initial concern for introducing Paul's thought to undergraduates is still evident in many of the illustrations and questions that I use, I hope that this small volume will also address the concerns and arouse the interest of adult laypeople, as well as seminarians who are studying Paul's theology at a more advanced level.

The book presumes a particular understanding of theology, and it is perhaps wise for me to articulate that assumption here. In my understanding, the language of theology interprets (and thus enables) human life by raising questions about what is of ultimate importance in human life and experience. That is, theology primarily concerns human life rather than doctrine. Doctrines are codifications of particular interpretations of human life in relation to the ultimate, or what we call God. In teaching a particular person's theology—as this volume attempts to do with the Apostle Paul—the goal is to show how the language and logic of the theologian help us interpret certain central aspects of human life and experience. This means, though, that we must not only mine the doctrine or particular language field of a theologian in order to understand his or her theology. We must also reflect critically upon human experience in order to understand how or whether that doctrine or language might reasonably be related to human life.

Thus, in the material that follows, I spend considerable time developing analogies drawn from our more or less common human experience in order to illustrate the experiential logic of Paul's thought. As teachers frequently do, I employ a personal voice in the hope that examples from my experience might encourage the readers to think critically about their own experience. (I urge readers to remember the essential fictive element in the pedagogical use of so-called personal experiences.) Numerous side-bars are designed to help the reader think critically about human life and relate such critical reflection to what Paul has to say about human life. Some may object that this introduces too much subjectivity into the intellectual enterprise. But critical reflection on experience would be better described as an effort to look objectively and publicly—that is, in conversation with others—at our own subjective experience and thus to widen our view of human existence. The goal in all these personal reflections is to lead the reader to think in a critical, rational way about our shared humanity.

The notion of a shared humanity is, of course, something of a problem in itself. I certainly do not pretend to define with any precision what such a notion might be. My goal is, rather, to lead the readers to think, preferably in conversation with other readers, about the similarities and differences between our particular experiences. How might we understand these experiences? To what extent—if at all—do they relate to Paul's understanding of human existence? Does Paul's thought shed any light on how we think about life in our world? Can we have an honest, critical, and fruitful conversation with Paul about the meaning of human experience?

Such an effort to relate Paul's thought to human life may, at first glance, appear to ignore some of the fundamental convictions of biblical scholarship today. Any careful biblical scholar is ever watchful of the tendency to import our own experience and expectations back onto our reading of the text. We must, so we are taught, distance ourselves from the text, for the text is, indeed, distant in time, space, and culture from us. To deny this distance is to engage in flagrant eisegesis—reading our own views or experience into the text rather than letting the text speak from its own foreign time and culture. This book will be sorely misunderstood if it is seen as an interpretation that ignores the cultural and historical difference between Paul's time and our own. I strongly urge readers to supplement their understanding of Paul with a study of some of the many excellent historical and sociological introductions to Paul and his world. The book presupposes such studies; it does not seek to replace them.

Rather, I have begun with the assumption that the classic thought systems of our Western cultures, those theologies or philosophies that have had and continue to have strong appeal and influence, have become classics because they continue to speak in meaningful ways to people across cultures, across time. It is certainly helpful to know something about fifth-century Athens when we study Plato, about early-twentieth-century Europe when we study Freud. But the thought of such masters, while rooted in and informed by such historical moments, transcends the limitations of their own time and space.

The thought systems (the theologies) of such people as John, Paul, or the ancient Israelite prophets are, I would argue, such classics within our Western world. While it is important for believing communities to understand these religious thinkers from the standpoint of their respective faiths, the thought of such religious giants has been so influential in our larger cultural context that they also deserve to be understood philosophically, if you will. That is, it is appropriate to ask the basic question, apart from the stance of a prior religious faith: Does Paul make sense? Is his thought logically coherent, and does it reflect what might be called an experiential logic? Is it a persuasive way to understand human life and experience? It is my conviction that Paul's theology does, indeed, make sense. I trust that readers of this volume will be challenged, if not to agree with Paul, at least to think about our human life together in critical and potent ways.

Many people have contributed directly and indirectly to the development of this book. I especially thank those who have been my mentors and conversation partners on Pauline matters over the years, Graydon F. Snyder and Robin Scroggs, as well as Nadine Pence Frantz, who during our many conversations has taught me much about the task of theology. Several colleagues have read earlier versions of the manuscript, and I especially thank Alexandra Brown, Philippa Carter, Robin Scroggs, and David Rhoads for their helpful critiques. I am grateful, as well, for the many friends and students who have offered suggestions, including my Wednesday Women's Seminar and the students in my classes at Muhlenberg College. I dedicate this book to my daughters, Ginny and Jaclyn Holsey. They continue to be my best teachers.

December 31, 1999
Coffeetown, Pennsylvania

Getting Started

Coming to Terms with the Apostle Paul

The purpose of this book is to introduce readers to the thought and theology of the Apostle Paul. Teaching courses on Paul for several years, I became increasingly discouraged at how difficult it is for nontheologians to come to terms with Paul and his writings. Still, often enough, experience encourages me that people are certainly capable of wrestling with Paul. The experience is far too rare, however, and much too random for my satisfaction. It is my hope that this book will afford a way into reading Paul's letters that will provide the nontheologian the opportunity to think with, and wrestle with, Paul's thought in a coherent way—to scan a fuller horizon of Paul's thought rather than settle for fragmentary glimpses.

OBSTACLES TO UNDERSTANDING PAUL'S THOUGHT

The obstacles to understanding Paul's writings and his thought are numerous, and at times seem insurmountable even to professionals. Some of these obstacles are present whenever we attempt to understand someone else's thought, especially a person from another historical period and another culture. But Paul presents his own particular obstacles as well.

An Unsystematic System

In the first place, Paul never systematically summarizes his thought, as did Plato or Aristotle, for instance. We know Paul's thought only through the few surviving letters that he wrote to the churches with which he was in contact. All of Paul's writings are occasional letters; that is, they were written on a specific occasion in order to address a specific problem at a specific time for a specific people. Presumably, he had an overall philosophy that led him to respond to problems in the ways that he did. But he never outlined this philosophy for us. Thus, we must extrapolate his general thought from the many, and often apparently conflicting, specific remarks. Yet it is difficult to understand his specific remarks without knowing something of his general thought. There is no way out of this circle—we must know both the general and the specific in order to know Paul's thought, but we can know the general only through the specific and can understand the specific only if we have some sense of the general.

This process of extrapolation is, however, not entirely foreign to us. All of life consists, to some degree, of drawing portraits of people and their character and their views from their reactions to a variety of situations. You might be able, for instance, to extrapolate my philosophy of parenting from my daily interactions with my children, or you might come to a fairly accurate sense of my philosophy of education by observing me teach in a variety of situations. In either of these instances I might, on occasion, say explicit things that come close to being a statement of my philosophy of parenting or education. But even these explicit statements are contextual, and it may be difficult to discern or to express accurately the relationships between such explicit statements.

Unfortunately, an introductory work like this cannot itemize all of Paul's occasional remarks closely enough in order for us to intuit the overall system. This book will provide something of a shortcut by setting forth a summary of my own extrapolation of Paul's philosophy of life, based on my own experience of studying Paul's interactions with his churches, as reflected in his letters.[1]

pels or the narratives of the Hebrew Bible is much easier than reading Paul, for we all basically understand how to read a story: There is a plot—a beginning, a middle, and an end (so Aristotle)—and there are characters. These things we readily recognize. But to many readers Paul's writing seems to go nowhere. His arguments are hard to follow; his transitions and emphases pass unnoticed. This is because Paul was trained both in Greco-Roman rhetoric and in rabbinic argument, and most modern readers do not have experience with either of these forms of writing. The purpose of rhetoric in the Greco-Roman world was to persuade. Education in the ancient world was primarily an education in rhetoric—how to recognize the way in which someone is trying to persuade you (i.e., how to listen wisely) and how to form a speech in order to persuade someone else (i.e., how to write and speak effectively). We learn early on in our culture the ploys of the advertising industry, how to read television commercials, for example. Unfortunately, however, we read Paul (and other authors from antiquity) the way a two-year-old watches commercials. We have not developed the critical-thinking skills to recognize when others are trying to persuade us, much less what strategies or devices they are using to get us to buy their product. The summary of Paul's thought provided in this work will enable the reader to make some sense of what Paul is talking about. A careful study of any of Paul's letters (or portions of the letters) needs to be supplemented by a basic introduction to how Paul uses standard rhetorical forms and devices.

The Problem of Rhetoric

A second obstacle to reading Paul lies in the form of his writing. Reading the Gos-

From Another Time and Place

We encounter the third obstacle to reading Paul successfully just as we would with any writer living in another time and place.

Our distance from Paul's time means that we must traverse several gaps between the then and the now. One such gap is the difference between Paul's culture(s) and our culture(s). We are outsiders when we read Paul; it is as though we were listening in to one side of a private conversation that draws on shared knowledge between the conversants. He refers to circumstances or to people or events that he assumes his readers know without needing explanation. But we do not know what he and they could assume. Paul and his readers shared certain assumptions about what it means to be human (anthropology), certain social expectations (sociology), and certain ways of imagining the world (mythology) that are foreign to us. He even writes in a language that is foreign to most of us. As Federico Fellini commented, "A different language is a different vision of life." Thus, I should not have been so surprised the first time I handed out a copy of Paul's one-page letter to his friend Philemon and the students declared that they could make no sense out of this letter at all. It is as though I threw them into a foreign country, without any experience in the culture or language, and expected them to pick up the nuances of the conversation between two people sitting on a park bench. Impossible, indeed!

Studying Paul, then, is a course in cross-cultural studies, to some degree. And unless we can (a) understand another culture, one that is different from our own, (b) traverse the gap (back and forth, back and forth) between the other and the self (which means we have some understanding of our own culture as culture, and not as "reality"), and (c) be willing to accept the inevitable misunderstandings that are a part of any conversation that strives for understanding (and truth), we will not be able to understand Paul's thought.

The primary purpose of this study is to introduce you to the thought of the Apostle Paul. Our goal is more like what you would find in a philosophy course than in a history course. But since, to understand someone's thought, we must perceive some of the context of their thinking, it will be necessary to say a few things about Paul's cultural and intellectual environment. Thus, each of the three parts of this book will be introduced by a chapter that sketches the chief intellectual issues that informed Paul's thought within his culture.[2]

The summary of Paul's thought that follows will draw on this basic cultural information. With this background in the intellectual and cultural issues at play in Paul's thought, I will then develop several analogies based on modern experiences of life in order to help you imagine what Paul might have intended. That is, I will draw on our shared cultural assumptions and experiences, though perhaps in new ways. My summary of Paul's thought can only be partial and provisional. I, too, must allow for the unavoidable misunderstandings when I attempt to understand someone from another time and place.

The "Terminological Gap"

The fourth obstacle to reading Paul lies in what I call the terminological gap, which is addressed most directly in this book. Paul uses several terms in his writings in an almost technical way. A solid grasp of Paul's definitions of these terms is essential to understanding his thought and his writings. It might be helpful here to distinguish between a *term* and a *word*.[3] Many of Paul's *words* are familiar to us: sin, law, Christ, body, flesh, believe, spirit. That is, we recognize these words and use them ourselves on occasion. But what we mean by these words usually differs markedly from what Paul meant by them. The problem, however, is not just that we define these words differently; these words also carry more weight for Paul than they do for us. When Paul uses the word *law,* for instance, there frequently lies behind this word a whole complex of ideas (and emotions) for which *law* is a shorthand expression. This is what I mean when I refer to Paul's *terms:* specific words that serve as a somewhat stable shorthand designation for a complex of ideas. Thus, in order to "come to terms" with Paul, we must understand Paul's terms; we must understand his technical vocabulary.[4]

These technical terms in Paul's vocabulary make him difficult to understand, not only because we may not recognize them as terms or because we may not know the meaning of those terms for Paul but, more importantly, because we often recognize the words but they mean something different to us than they did to Paul. This is especially true for those who have grown up in a religious context, and even more true for those who have grown up in a Christian church. We have been taught the meaning of these words, or at least we know how to use them correctly. But I wager a safe bet that what we mean when we use these words is not what Paul meant. Indeed, in some instances, our use of these words can almost prevent us from understanding Paul's quite foreign use. In short, these terms are common words with uncommon meanings.

Therefore, the task of coming to terms with Paul necessitates that we not only learn some things but simultaneously unlearn some things. We must both remember and forget. It is perhaps impossible to forget in this sense, however. And so we must move back and forth, as it were, between Paul's definitions of these terms and our own previous definitions of them, contrasting the former with the latter. We must play on Paul's field and ours simultaneously—and this is hard intellectual work. It is also at times hard

emotional work because our education in these words—that is, our religious education—is deeply related to the things that we hold dearest in life. Good, rigorous, intelligent thought about things that matter to us is unavoidably connected with our emotions. To deny this healthy and necessary connection is to deny the profound importance of intellectual thought.

This study focuses on this task—coming to terms with Paul. The following chapters define four major terms in Paul's thought: *righteousness, law, sin,* and *Christ.* The terms are interdependent, and you will find it of high value to reread the earlier chapters after you have finished the study.

The treatment of each term varies according to the subject matter and because of the constraints of laying out Paul's thought in a linear manner. The discussions of *righteousness* and *law* will lay the groundwork and background for Paul's thought. They will focus on the Jewish presuppositions of Paul's theology. In this material most citations will be from the Hebrew Bible. The second part presents several interrelated aspects of Paul's understanding of *sin,* including the notions of slavery and death. Paul's notion of sin is necessarily related to his Jewish understanding. But in his discussions on sin, Paul also shows evidence of sharing some similar concerns with the Greco-Roman philosophers. Thus, this section will begin by briefly introducing Paul's Greco-Roman context. The third and final part of the book addresses the most complex term that Paul uses: *Christ.* Here it will become evident that Paul has taken a decisive turn in his thought—one that entails a certain redefinition of the earlier terms. Along the way we will need to attend to several terms that relate to Paul's understanding of Christ, for example, *justification, grace, faith, hope, spirit,* and *resurrection.* In this extended discussion of Paul's experience of Christ, we begin to see how Paul uses his tradition regarding righteousness and law in creative ways and in response to the Greco-Roman situation in order to articulate a new understanding of law, righteousness, and sin.

The Experiential Dimension of Paul's Thought

I spoke in the last sentence about Paul's experience of Christ. It is clear throughout Paul's letters that his thought was integrally related to his experience. Paul was not a thinker who presumed that he was a mere objective observer of reality. His thought was unabashedly experiential—he was attempting to understand his experience and to assist the churches in understanding their experience. Paul's theology is a theology for adults. That is, Paul's thought depends upon his own life experience, and we can only understand Paul's thought if we have experienced life. This may be overstating the case, but it is nevertheless crucial to acknowledge at the outset that Paul's intellectual project consisted, in large part, of his efforts to understand his (and others') human experience.

There was a time when I thought that the difficulty I had in teaching Paul effectively at the undergraduate level was related to the relative inexperience of young-adult students. It is, of course, true that college-age students have experienced less of life than a forty-year-old adult has. But I suspect the problem is not lack of experience so much as it is the lack of opportunity the students have had to reflect critically on their own experience. If we have not had the opportunity to name our experience, then we are unable to claim that experience as our own. Since theological thinking demands some awareness of how philosophical thought and personal experience are necessarily related, throughout each chapter I will ask the reader

to think about her or his own experience—to name the experience. In addition, each of the book's three parts closes with a section entitled *Making Connections*. These exercises suggest activities that will enable readers to make connections between human experience and the theological ideas presented in the preceding chapters.

It is my hope that the format of this book and the study of Paul's reflection on his life experience will give you the opportunity to reflect critically on your own life experience. Perhaps Paul's reflections will be helpful; or perhaps, by disagreeing with Paul's reflections, you can claim your own different experience in strengthening ways.

THE VALUE OF STUDYING PAUL'S THOUGHT

Despite all the sometimes formidable obstacles to reading and understanding the Apostle Paul, despite all my frustrations and failures when trying to teach Paul's thought in an undergraduate context—to Christians, Jews, Muslims, and others—I have grown in my conviction that a study of Paul's thought can be a valuable exercise in a multifaith, pluralistic context and can help us understand how we live together in a larger society.

Building Critical-thinking Skills

Studying the complexity and coherence of Paul's thought and specialized vocabulary affords a prime opportunity to hone critical-thinking skills. This text is not written strictly for followers of Christ—though I trust that those who consider themselves Christians will find new encouragement for their faith. The more I study Paul, the more I become convinced that his thought is worth studying, even if one does not make any sort of faith commitment to adopt his thought as one's own. That is, you do not have to be a Platonist in order to value a study of Plato, or a Marxist to enjoy and learn from a study of *Das Kapital.* You do not have to make the religious commitment to Paul's interpretation of reality in order to appreciate his intellectual achievement.

Interacting with Another Culture

Another value of an academic study of Paul's writings lies in his cultural distance from us. The foreignness of Paul and his world presents a rich opportunity to struggle to understand another culture by creatively pursuing ways to traverse the gap between that culture and our own. A full study of Paul's letters necessitates that we grapple with the everyday realities of another time and place—a time and a place where people lived in very different circumstances than we do, and where they thought and believed and "knew" ideas that are quite foreign to us. Although we can never fully know a person or a culture that is truly foreign to us, we can nevertheless learn how to make sense of the things in their world that seem peculiar to us. Meeting new people always affords an opportunity to expand our own limited horizons. We discover new experiences and new ways of thinking about old problems. And beginning this cross-cultural conversation can perhaps offer us new possibilities for moving in creative ways in our own culture, for no living culture is stagnant.

Thinking Theologically: Connecting Intellect and Experience

The experiential dimensions of Paul's thought can also provide a valuable occasion for us to wrestle with the ways that the intellect, our experience, and our emotions interconnect whenever we are discussing questions of meaning and value. Again, this is not to insist that Paul's meaning and value are the right ones. Rather, the ways that Paul thinks about his own experience (and that of his churches) can be a catalyst for us to reflect critically and intelligently on our experiences in life.

Throughout this study I will use a variety of illustrations drawn from our actual present experience. Their primary purpose is to help us understand Paul's language and thought. But the illustrations may function in a second way as well. We live in a different world from that of the Apostle Paul. Many in our world find it difficult to believe in a personal God or to care much about a relationship with such a God.[5] For such people, all this God-talk that Paul does may seem to be unimportant at best, and so much nonsense at worst. One of the things I suggest by using these illustrations is that Paul's God-talk—that is, his theology—is a potentially useful analysis of human relationships and human identity, and this is true even if one cannot buy into Paul's whole mythological world.

The problems Paul analyzes under the rubric of *sin* and its relation to law, for example, are problems that we all face. Stated in its most basic way, the problem is, How do we deal with the authority figures who contribute to our lives? Whether I believe in God or not, I nevertheless have to wrestle with how I am going to relate to my parents, to those people who have fostered my life. As many will attest, this is a problem that is hardly resolved in our teens or our twenties. Perhaps most people carry this problem into their forties, their sixties, and beyond. Indeed, the problem goes beyond that of dealing with our parents. As we go through life, we adopt other authority figures—people whom we emulate and yet over against whom we also need to define ourselves. Human happiness, fulfillment, and maturity are somehow integrally connected with coming to terms—in creative ways—with the people and places and institutions that have formed us both psychologically and sociologically. If I mix the language of illustration with that of Paul, I might say it this way: Maturity (righteousness) consists in coming to terms with our Creator—whoever that Creator might be. We do not have to believe in the story of *Oedipus Rex* in order to find Freud's analysis of the Oedipus complex compelling. Nor is it necessary to believe in Paul's mythology of God and Christ to find value in his analysis of a common and complex human difficulty.

My hope is that, by using these kinds of illustrations, you can begin to understand theology as a fruitful way of thinking about human life. If the God-language gets in the way of your understanding the dynamics of what Paul is saying, the illustrations allow you to shift to a human analogy and think about it on that level. The God-language can then become a potent shorthand enabling

you to explore the dynamics of human experience—both your own and that of others. Theology is an intellectual language that seeks to articulate something of the ultimate in our human experience. It is a structure of thought that helps us think carefully about the ultimate questions and commitments of human existence: What are we? Why are we? How can we live? How do we die? Thus, the critical nexus of intellect, experience, and emotion in Paul's theology not only can be a fertile ground for learning to think about our own past experience; it also can enable us to make decisions about the future intelligently.

In short, a prime value of studying Paul that will, I trust, emerge in this study is that of coming to a better understanding of the relationship between critical thought and ethics, between thinking well and living well. Thus, the goals of this book mirror my own teaching and life objective: To live thoughtfully, we must be thought-full persons.

part one

Paul's Jewish Heritage

A Righteous God

Many of us have grown up hearing about Paul's "conversion" to Christianity. We forget that Paul was a Jew. More important, we fail to recognize that Paul was always a Jew. Christianity, in the sense of an established religion, did not exist during Paul's lifetime. Yet Paul did talk a great deal about Jesus Christ. How confusing to us today to hear about a religious Jew who spent so much time thinking and writing about the hero of Christianity, Jesus! It will be important at the beginning of our study, then, to practice this new kind of learning, where we simultaneously learn and unlearn some things. For, in order to learn about Paul's Jewish heritage and message, we will have to forget our assumptions about the nature of Judaism and Christianity. At the end of this chapter you should be able to list at least three things that characterize Paul's Judaism, as well as describe some of the differences between the Judaism and Christianity of today and the various Judaisms of the first century.

1

Paul the Jew

"I Am a Hebrew"

What does it mean for us to say that Paul was a Jew? Paul himself tells us that he was an ethnic Jew, that he was born to Jewish parents. He says that he was "of the people of Israel, of the tribe of Benjamin, a Hebrew born of Hebrews" (Phil 3:5). Not only was he born of Jewish parents, however; he also was a member of the religious community of Judaism: "circumcised on the eighth day" and trained as a Pharisee.[1] In his young adulthood, Paul says, he "persecuted the church of God violently and tried to destroy it" (Gal 1:13). But something changed Paul's mind about this Jewish movement that he called "the church of God." He became not only supportive of it; he became one of its primary spokespersons. Here's what Paul said about this change of mind:

> He who had set me apart before I was born, and . . . called me through his grace, was pleased to reveal his Son to me, in order that I might preach him among the Gentiles. (Gal 1:15–16)

Paul did not "convert" to Christianity. No, his change of mind had nothing to do with leaving one religion in order to follow a different God. The God of his people—the God of Israel—had "called" him to preach to the Gentiles concerning the Son of the God of Israel. Paul was an apostle[2] of the Jewish God, sent out to preach among the Gentiles. Paul was calling the Gentiles to worship the God of Israel.

PAUL'S JEWISH PROCLAMATION

Paul was a Jew who lived among non-Jews. Except for short periods, Paul lived his life as a Diaspora Jew.[3] While some Jews of the Diaspora did try to blend in with the surrounding Greco-Roman population, it is clear from Paul's own writings that—both before and after he threw his lot in with those who called Jesus the Christ—Paul was firmly committed to his Jewish heritage and to living out his life in faithfulness to his understanding of this heritage.

It seems odd to us today that this person, who has been called the second founder of Christianity, was neither Christian nor Gentile. Paul was a Jew: He worshiped the God of Israel, lived out of and in relation to the history and traditions of the Jewish people, and held anticipations for the future that were deeply informed by his Jewish heritage.

The God of Israel

Those of us who live in Western societies are accustomed to assuming that there is only one God. To be a monotheist in our day and time and in this Western world is both to accept the dominant cultural assumptions about the nature of the divine and to express an enlightened tolerance for religious diversity. Such was not the case, however, for Paul and other Jews in antiquity.

To state it bluntly: To be a monotheist in the Greco-Roman world demanded a rejection of the dominant culture and of the religious confessions of one's neighbors. By contrast, the defining religious confession of the Jews does not seem to represent any daring spirit of confrontation.

> Hear, O Israel: The LORD is our God, the LORD alone. (Deut 6:4)

When all are agreed that there is but one true God, this basic confession of the Jews seems almost commonplace. Perhaps even to those Jews in Paul's day who by chance lived well-protected and provincial lives firmly within an all-Jewish community, this confession of the oneness of God seemed obvious and constituted no challenge, either for oneself or for one's neighbors. But if, like Paul, you were a Jew who lived in the Diaspora, as a member of a minority population within Greco-Roman society, such a confession was curious at least, and radical and confrontational at most.

Two related factors within Greco-Roman society lent such a curious and even radical context to the Jewish confession of the oneness of God. First, Greco-Roman society was "populated with gods." Every city boasted a multitude of temples, each temple to a different god or goddess. For a Jew to say solemnly, "There is one God," when any observant soul could walk through the city and see prominent and manifold evidence to the contrary was at the very least odd. In our day, were we to assert that there were many gods and goddesses, we would have a real argument on our hands. We would be asked to offer proof. Why, even people of different religions—Jews, Christians, Muslims—acknowledge that they worship the same God! The currency of the United States, for example, implicitly acknowledges the singularity of God: "In God We Trust." There is no need to name the god, to designate which god we trust. There is—this is our culture's assumption—only one God. But in Paul's society the situation would be just the reverse. The culture assumed that there were multiple gods and goddesses. To trust in a God, one would need to be explicit: In which deity do you trust? Thus, to assert that there is only one deity was, in itself, countercultural.

This countercultural religious affirmation of the Jews was also a radical, and some might say intolerant, stance to take within the pluralistic society of the Roman Empire. For not only did the Greeks and Romans accept that there were many different gods and goddesses; they assumed that one's religious life would consist of worshiping several of these deities. That is, Greco-Roman religions were, generally speaking, not exclusivistic in character. An individual might be active in the civic cult, maintain certain household gods, and participate in one or more of the mystery religions. The religions' gods and goddesses did not demand that

---

1:1 Thinking about God

Since much of what we will be studying here speaks of God, it might be good for you to take a few minutes to sort through some of your assumptions about God and religion.

1. Do you believe there is only one God and all religious people worship the same God? Why or why not?
2. If you are an atheist or agnostic, what is it about "God" that you don't believe?
3. Finally, see if you can define your concept of God. That is, what makes God God?

---

their devotees be exclusively committed to them.

In contrast to this religious openness, the God of Israel demanded Israel's exclusive worship. This God declares, "I the LORD your God am a jealous God" (Exod 20:5). Israel was to worship no other God but YHWH.[4] To do so was to violate the covenant that Israel had made with this God at Sinai. The Greeks and the Romans might play the field, but Israel's God demanded faithful religious monogamy. Thus, the Jews' declaration that God was one, that their God was the only true God, constituted an implicit, if not an explicit, judgment on the religious beliefs and practices of their neighbors. Further, to deny that YHWH was the only God, or to suggest that YHWH was not a single God, would be to reject the very foundation of Judaism. To be a Jew meant—at the very least—to worship solely the God of Israel. The Jewish religious life was defined solely in relation to this God.

Thus, Paul was Jewish: He maintained his faith in, and his relation to, this one God, YHWH. "For us there is one God, the Father, from whom are all things and for whom we exist" (1 Cor 8:6). It was this God and no other that Paul preached. Yes, he preached Jesus Christ. But this preaching centered around the proclamation that God—that is, the God of Israel—had raised this Jesus from the dead. Paul, like any other faithful Jew, re-

jected the existence of other gods and goddesses. He insisted, as had his Jewish ancestors, on the exclusive worship of the one true God. Throughout, his thought depends upon this assumption: There is one true God, the God of Israel, the God of Abraham and Sarah, of Isaac and Jacob, the God of the Jews.

The Traditions of Israel

Each of us is informed by the culture in which we live. This is a commonplace. But what is frequently missed is that most of us are surrounded by several different cultures. There is no monolithic, monochrome Culture. This fact is especially obvious for those who are minorities. An African-American surely knows this, as do Latinos/Latinas or Asian-Americans. Even the name indicates the cultural plurality: African and American; Asian and American. These multiple ethnic and national identities cause explosions among us. What does it mean to be African? To be American? To be African-American? Which identity informs you when you are a person of multiple identities? From which culture do you derive your script for how to live life, for how to think about life?

The issue of cultural plurality was alive in Paul's world as well. It was certainly an issue for Jews who lived as a minority within Greco-Roman society. According to whose script should a Diaspora Jew live? Are Ho-

1:2 Your Cultural Traditions

1. Citizens of particular countries share certain cultural traditions. See if you can identify things that you share with other citizens of your country.

    a. common stories
    b. common heroes
    c. common holidays

2. Are you also aware of cultural traditions you share with others of your particular ethnic heritage? Give some examples.

3. Although the Americans and the British share the English language, we sometimes use different words to refer to the same thing. What, for example, is a "lift" in England? Can you think of other examples where our terminology differs?

mer and Socrates models for Jews as well as for Greeks? Or do Abraham and Moses define a Jew—even a Jew who lives among the Greeks? For Paul, at any rate, the answer is clear. Paul persistently draws his material from the history and literature of Israel, rather than from the history or literature of Greece. He did not aim to translate the Jewish faith into the terms of Greek philosophy or relate this faith to Roman history. This Apostle to the Gentiles brought his own history and traditions and literature to the Gentiles. He wanted to communicate the richness of his own faith to the Gentiles and to include them in his own heritage. He spoke and wrote in the Greek language, but the vocabulary of his Greek reflects the thought and story of Israel.

All of the key terms that we will be studying are key terms within Judaism, and Paul's thinking about these terms is informed by that Jewish conversation. Thus, although Greeks had long valued righteousness as a virtue and as a necessity of justice, Paul does not emphasize this virtue of righteousness but, rather, invokes the "righteousness of God"—that is, the God of Israel. Greeks and Romans had law—both in legal systems and in cultural traditions—but Paul's discussion about the law derives from his reflections on the Jewish law, the Torah. Similarly, for Paul sin is a barrier that erodes one's relationship with YHWH, while for the Greek philosophers a sin is simply a mistake (albeit sometimes a serious mistake). And *Christ* is a word that is taken directly from Jewish thought; it is simply the Greek translation of the Hebrew for "Messiah."

Thus, any understanding of Paul's thought requires that we learn something about the history and tradition of Israel. The next two chapters narrate something of this history and illustrate some of the logic of the thought that had emerged in this tradition. As we move through succeeding sections, we will see how this basic foundation within Judaism informed Paul's interaction with the Gentiles and how his interaction with the Gentiles cast new questions for him to address to his own traditions.

The Expectations of Israel

It was not, however, only Israel's past that determined Paul's thought. Paul also claimed from his Jewish culture Israel's expectations for the future. These expectations have been given a technical name by scholars: apocalyptic eschatology. *Eschatology* means "the study of last things." That is, eschatology deals with the end of time: What will happen at the end of history—both corporate human history and individual human life? Whenever you talk about subjects such as heaven or hell, reincarnation or an afterlife, you are (although you probably didn't know this) engaging in an eschatological discussion.

Apocalyptic eschatology is a particular kind of eschatological thinking that focuses on at least two items. First, apocalyptic thinking assumes that some crisis will bring this present world to an end and inaugurate a new world. Second, it emphasizes the cosmic nature and purpose of the crisis, rather than just an individual (or national) transformation. Perhaps a comparison with other types of eschatology will help to illustrate these features of apocalyptic eschatology.

The simplest type of eschatology may be called promise-fulfillment eschatology. Something is promised and then the promise is fulfilled. Imagine that you become engaged. You are then living "eschatologically"—in anticipation of the marriage. You have received a promise that will be fulfilled in due time as things follow their natural course.

Illustration 1
Promise-Fulfillment Eschatology

Promise —————————▶ *Fulfillment*

Promise-fulfillment eschatology is a simple eschatology
that asserts that what has been promised in the
past will be fulfilled in the future.

Such is the case in the earliest experience of Israel. God promises that Israel will enter the land of Canaan and will live in a "land flowing with milk and honey" (Exod 3:7–8). God

has promised, and Israel agrees with this promise of God (Exod 19:3–8). And Israel does, indeed, arrive at the land of Canaan (Joshua).

But just as might happen in a marriage, the Israelites' arrival in the land of Canaan did not prove to be quite the fulfillment that they had anticipated. Imagine that, after the engaged couple marry, now living on the promise of "love, honor, and cherish," they begin to have marital difficulties. The fulfillment is somehow escaping them. What do they do? Well, they may decide to go to a minister or a therapist for counseling. And if the counseling is helpful, the spouses can return to renew their vows, their promise to love, honor, and cherish each other. This type of eschatology recognizes that things are not quite so simple as promise-fulfillment. Life is complicated and difficult, and we frequently need to return to the original promise and reaffirm it.

Such was the message of Israel's prophets. They proclaimed that the people had failed to experience the fulfillment of the promise because they had neglected to attend to the original promise.

> And I brought you into a plentiful land
>   to enjoy its fruits and its good things.
> But when you came in you defiled my land,
>   and made my heritage an abomination.
>   (Jer 2:7)

Thus, because Israel veered away from the original promise that God and Israel had made (Exod 19:3–8), it now received this word:

> Return, faithless Israel, says the LORD. I will not look on you in anger, for I am merciful, says the LORD. I will not be angry forever. Only acknowledge your guilt. . . . Return, O faithless children, says the LORD. (Jer 3:12–14)

Thus, we might call this promise-return-fulfillment eschatology a prophetic eschatology.

Illustration 2
Prophetic Eschatology

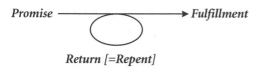

Promise ⟶ *Fulfillment*

Return [=Repent]

Prophetic eschatology recognizes that life sometimes veers
off course and away from the fulfillment. Repentance is
necessary in order to return to the original promise and
be "back on track" toward the fulfillment.

But, alas, what happens when you return
and return and return and simply can't ever
seem to stay on track, much less arrive at the
fulfillment? In the case of a marriage—at least
in our society—this frequently means that the
married couple get a divorce. Whatever the
legal arrangements, however, it is certainly clear
that a crisis has been reached. The fulfillment
of the promise is unattainable through repetitious efforts to return to the original promise.
It becomes clear that some kind of break is
necessary; and perhaps on the other side of this
shattering crisis, there will emerge a new hope,
a new possibility for fulfillment.

Illustration 3
Apocalyptic Eschatology

Promise   *Crisis*   *Fulfillment*

Apocalyptic eschatology emerges when efforts to repent
appear to be ineffectual. Because there are mighty forces
at work that prevent fulfillment, a crisis develops. Some
outside force intervenes and destroys the situation
where repentance has become ineffectual and inaugurates
a new situation with fulfillment that would have been
impossible within the original situation.

The history of the Jewish people had not
been a happy one. Indeed, it had been a very

difficult and trying history. For only two
short periods in their existence had they
been a truly independent people. The texture
of their lives was determined by foreign rulers. And now, half a millennium later, the
promise was still not fulfilled. They still lived
in subservience to others. Even their repentance did not seem to be sufficient.

The world and its rulers were powerful
and destructive. The trauma of Israel's failure to know the fulfillment of God's promise
was so great that Israel's prophets turned to
using fantastic language to describe the helplessness of their situation. (See the text of
Zechariah in sidebar 1:3.) Just as shows like
Star Trek imagine evil forces as strange creatures such as the Borg, so Israel's prophets
resorted to bizarre images (e.g., the four
horns in Zechariah) to describe the forces
in the world that thwarted the fulfillment
of God's promise. But just as the starship *Enterprise* always wins in the end, so Israel's
prophets proclaimed that God would bring a
dramatic destruction of those evil forces and
bring fulfillment to Israel.

Only the cosmic power of God could
alter this impossible situation. The fulfillment would come as apocalypse—as catas-
trophe and as new fulfillment. Israel waited
for a Messiah, who would rule Israel in God's
kingdom. When that day arrived, the entire
cosmos would be the realm of God. The creation in all its parts would, at long last,
honor the Creator.

This, then, was the apocalyptic expectation of the Jews—and of Paul. The future is
in God's hands. The fate of Israel, of the
world, indeed of the entire cosmos, will be
determined by a great action of God, wherein
God will establish God's own sovereignty
once again over all creation. The Messiah
will be the herald and sign of that apocalyptic
moment. This was Paul's expectation for the
future.

1:3   An Apocalyptic Prophet

The Lord Conquers Evil—

And I lifted my eyes and saw, and behold, four horns! And I said to the angel who talked with me, "What are these?" And he answered me, "These are the horns which have scattered Judah, Israel, and Jerusalem." Then the LORD showed me four smiths. And I said, "What are these coming to do?" He answered, "These are the horns which scattered Judah, so that no man raised his head; and these have come to terrify them, to cast down the horns of the nations who lifted up their horns against the land of Judah to scatter it." (Zech 1:18–21)

God's People Rejoice—

Sing and rejoice, O daughter of Zion; for lo, I come and I will dwell in the midst of you, says the LORD. And many nations shall join themselves to the LORD in that day, and shall be my people; and I will dwell in the midst of you, and you shall know that the LORD of hosts has sent me to you. And the LORD will inherit Judah as his portion in the holy land, and will again choose Jerusalem.

Be silent, all flesh, before the LORD; for he has roused himself from his holy dwelling.
(Zech 2:10–13)

WORSHIPING THE GOD OF ISRAEL: THEN AND NOW

One of the reasons a study of Paul's thought can be challenging to us today is that we live in a different culture than did Paul. The section above on Paul's Jewish heritage provides a basic introduction to the intellectual heritage of a Jew such as Paul in the first century. But another factor complicates our attempt to hear Paul's thought: Although our culture(s) today is significantly different from that of Paul, it has itself been influenced both by Paul himself and by the larger heritage within which Paul stood. We know today, for instance, what it means to be a Jew or to believe in Christ. Many of us continue to worship the God of Israel. Yet the twenty centuries that separate us from Paul and the Judaism of the first century have wrought some significant changes in Judaism, as well as in what came to be called Christianity.

Judaism: Then and Now

Although we cannot at this juncture take the luxury of describing or analyzing the complexity of first-century Judaism, a few comments may highlight some of the differences between the Judaism of Paul's day and that of our own. For one thing, the Judaism of Paul's day might more accurately be described as Judaisms than as a singular Judaism. That is, the centuries around the turn of the era (third century B.C.E. to second century C.E.) were volatile ones for the Jews who lived throughout the Roman Empire and beyond. Even in Palestine there were several different ways of being Jewish, that is, of understanding what it meant to be Jewish. Many thinkers were attempting to define Judaism, and these different definitions competed with one another. Paul's "Christianity" was, during these early days of the first century, yet one more attempt to define Judaism.[5]

1:4 Thinking Eschatologically

The text has illustrated eschatology with the example of the future that marriage can provide. See if you can apply these three types of eschatology to other examples of hope for the future.

1. Imagine that someone told you that you would get a better-paying job if you went to college and got a degree. Explain what the following eschatologies might look like in relation to going to college (the promise) and getting a job (the fulfillment).

   a. promise-fulfillment eschatology
   b. prophetic eschatology
   c. apocalyptic eschatology

2. Eschatology, however, ultimately has more to do with corporate and cosmic expectations. See if you can describe different eschatologies for the environment of the earth. To get you started:

   a. promise-fulfillment eschatology: if we take care of the earth, then the earth will last forever
   b. prophetic eschatology
   c. apocalyptic eschatology

With all these different and competing definitions of Judaism, what held the various Judaisms of the first century together in one unit? The temple in Jerusalem. To be sure, the different varieties of Judaism maintained different views about the centrality of the temple. But its—and Jerusalem's—physical existence functioned, in some ways, as the unquestioned core of Judaism.[6] Thus, the destruction of the temple by the Romans in 70 C.E. constituted a major crisis for Jews throughout the ancient world. One of the significant consequences of this crisis was the establishment of an academy at Yavneh, a city near the Mediterranean coast in Palestine, where some key Jewish leaders gathered together in 90 C.E. to redefine Judaism in a world without a temple and without a physical center in Jerusalem.

The Judaism that resulted from the efforts of these rabbis at the academy of Yavneh is frequently called rabbinic Judaism. This eventually came to serve as the founda-tion of all the later Judaism in the West. The academy determined the canon of the Jewish Scriptures, or Tanak. Its leaders maintained the earliest parts of the oral traditions that were eventually codified in the Talmud. It was also at this academy that the primary locus of Jewish worship and ritual shifted to the home (since the temple was now destroyed).

For our purposes, it is important to re-member that rabbinic Judaism served as the source for all varieties of Judaism after the first century. It did not, however, serve as the source for Paul's Judaism—for the simple reason that Paul died before the destruction of the temple and before the academy at Yavneh. Thus, when we say, "Paul was a Jew," we do not mean that he was a Jew like the Jews who worship in synagogues today. The Judaism that Paul practiced still had a temple and temple sacrifices. His Judaism had not yet given final canonical form to its Scriptures, and thus many other Jewish writings were, during Paul's day, considered quasi-scriptural.[7] But if Paul did not worship or live as a Jew in the same ways that Jews worship or live today, neither was Paul a Christian in the same ways that people are Christians today.

Paul's Faith in Christ and Christianity Today

Paul was a Jew who believed that Jesus of Nazareth was the Christ—a simple statement that conceals great complexity. For just as Paul's Judaism was different from the Judaism of today, so Paul's "Christianity" was quite different from any of the multitude of expressions of Christianity today. The differences between Paul's faith and practice and those of Christians today are many. Fortunately, for the purposes of the present study, we do not need to delineate them all. Here, however, are a few of the things that most Christians in the West take for granted today but that Paul would never have known:

1. The classical definitions of the Trinity and the nature of Christ were not formulated until three or four centuries after Paul lived. The language and thought of the Nicene and Chalcedonian creeds would have been quite foreign to Paul.

2. Paul's churches were not public institutions with any social power or influence. They were small, socially marginal groups of people who, to a greater or lesser extent, associated with the Jewish synagogues. Indeed, it would be two centuries and more before the Christian churches would be recognized as a legitimate religion in the Roman Empire.

3. The organization of the churches of Paul's day was very fluid and undefined. There were no formal buildings (the groups met in homes), no ordained ministry, and no established liturgy.

4. Finally, the New Testament had not yet been written. Paul himself wrote letters that would, in the coming centuries, be considered by Christians to be Scripture. His letters are the earliest of the writings making up the New Testament, which means Paul had not read any of the Gospels, because none had yet been written!

Even if these four items were the only differences between the faith and practice of Christians today and those of Paul, the effects would be astonishing. Simply put, Paul would recognize almost nothing of the ways that Christians talk and worship today.

These differences do not mean, however, that Paul would necessarily disagree with all the practices or language of Christianity today. But we must be very careful about assuming that "Paul was a Christian." Paul did believe that Israel's God had revealed himself in Jesus, the Christ. And Paul called others, both Jew and Gentile, to share in this belief. Those who shared this experience with Paul were not called Christians but believers.[8] When Paul addressed his letters to these believers, he called them simply "the saints." They, too, in Paul's view, were followers of the Jewish God, believers that the God of Israel had been revealed in Jesus of Nazareth, who was the Christ.

CONCLUSION

Our aim is to understand the thought of the Apostle Paul. Any philosophy or theology is, in some sense, a map of the world. It is an attempt to describe what the world is and how to move about in that world effectively. How do we find our way together in this world? How do we negotiate the terrain of life, recognizing the significant landmarks, the obstacles, and the good land? If we are to "read the map" of Paul's thought, we need to be able to understand his language and his symbols. This chapter has sought to provide background to the language and symbols that Paul uses as he draws his "map of the world."

A study of Paul's map drawing can be particularly fruitful for anyone who wishes to understand Western thought better, because Paul stood at a critical juncture in Western religious history. When "Christianity" was not yet Christianity but still a form of Judaism, there stood Paul, revising the maps of Judaism at his disposal, using the language and symbols from his Jewish heritage to redescribe his world. The map that Paul sketched out as he worked among these "saints" provided the intellectual foundation for what would eventually be a new religion. Paul drew, then, a particularly potent map of the world. It has influenced generations of thinkers (both positively and negatively) and has become one of the fundamental intellectual structures of the West.

READING CHECK:

☑ Why was the Jewish affirmation of the oneness of God a radical statement in the Greco-Roman society of the first century?

☑ From what culture did Paul draw his major examples and stories?

☑ Define apocalyptic eschatology.

☑ How was the Judaism of Paul's day different from the Judaism of today?

☑ How did Paul's "Christianity" differ from Christian experience and belief today?

This chapter describes the Jewish view of righteousness that Paul presupposes in his thought. Thus, most of the biblical citations will be from the Hebrew Bible (what Christians call the Old Testament), rather than from Paul himself. In part 3 we will return to this description of righteousness and see how Paul applied it to his own understanding of the role of Christ, who was, in Paul's view, the revelation of God's righteousness. In order to understand how Paul could argue that Christ was such a revelation, we must first understand what Paul presupposes about righteousness.

As you read this chapter, look for three definitions of righteousness. Mark them clearly in the margins of the text. After reading the chapter, you should be able to identify these definitions and explain the relationships between them.

2

Righteousness

The Power of God

"Oh, she thinks she's so righteous!" A study that begins with a discussion of the word *righteousness* is not likely to arouse much excitement in us, for in our general vocabulary *righteous* does not have particularly positive overtones. We can and do use *righteous* or *righteousness* in a positive way to describe a good person—that is, a person who does good things. But more frequently the term carries connotations for us of self-righteousness. At least on the street (rather than in church or synagogue), our exclamation "Oh, she's so righteous" tends to identify the poor soul who is the object of the conversation as something of a Goody Two-shoes at best, a hypocrite at worst.

Hence, as we begin our experiment of attempting to understand Paul—a foreign man in a foreign world—we are immediately confronted with a clash of definitions. For if in our world the word *righteousness* carries a somewhat distasteful meaning, in the world

of Paul and his Jewish contemporaries *righteousness* denoted the greatest hope and joy of human life. The goal of this chapter is, then, twofold: first, to lay out a definition of righteousness that can be understood intellectually; but second (and perhaps more important), to enable us to understand effectively some of the positive associations with the term *righteousness.*

PEACE ON EARTH

God's goal for the cosmos is shalom—peace. Peace can be described as the absence of enmity: The lion and the lamb lie down together (Isa 11:6); warring humans "beat their swords into ploughshares" (Isa 2:4). Stated positively, shalom is that existence in which everything fits together—a good place for everything, and everything in its place. Shalom is order; it is right-relatedness; it is wholeness. Shalom is the integrity of the whole—of the whole created cosmos, of everything that is.

To state it most simply, God's righteousness is God's active bringing together of the whole of the created order. God's righteousness is God's shalom-making activity. This assumes that the world is not in peace, is not at peace. And God intends to put the world at peace, to "peace" the world together.

With God *righteousness* is an action word. It does not primarily describe a quality or a characteristic of God. To describe God by saying, "God is righteous," is something like describing ourselves by saying, "I am a teacher," or, "You are a student." I am a teacher because I teach. And you are students because you study. Getting a graduate degree in New Testament did not make me a teacher. I am only a teacher if I teach—if I engage in the activity of teaching. Enrolling in a university or casually reading a book does not make you a student. You are only a student if you study—if you engage in the activity of studying. When we assert that God is righteous, we claim—if we are using Paul's

vocabulary—that God is actively engaged in putting the world together. Righteousness is a characteristic of God only insofar as it describes the fundamental action of God in relation to the cosmos.

Paul and the Judaism within which Paul was nurtured affirmed resolutely that God is righteous. By this they meant that YHWH, the God the Jews worshiped, acts to bring about shalom—to put the world together. But immediately upon hearing such an affirmation, we hit upon our first problem—one that will occupy us throughout this study. If God is righteous, and if God's righteousness is God's activity of putting the world together, then God, it appears, is not doing a very good job! Indeed, we might be tempted to claim—on the grounds of the proposition's logic so far—that God is unrighteous. At the very least, we would have to admit that God's righteous activity is not very effective.

Our world certainly does not look like it is coming together; rather, many of us fear that precisely the opposite is happening. In Tucumcari, New Mexico, a janitor named

---

2:1 Where Is Shalom?

1. Which of the following three statements best reflects your view?

   _____ a. The world is getting better all the time. I anticipate that the human situation will be better one hundred years from now than it is today.

   _____ b. The world is basically the same as it has always been. Our problems today are not significantly different from what they have been throughout history.

   _____ c. The world is getting worse and worse. We face more serious problems in our world today than the world has ever known, and it doesn't look like it is ever going to get any better.

2. Write a short paragraph explaining why you chose the statement you did. Be sure to include reflection about whether you think this statement holds true for all of the world or just for our own culture. Do you think there may be cultures elsewhere in the world that you might evaluate differently?

Jake in my dad's church used a delightful expression, one that my mother quickly adopted, and so I have heard and used it all my life. If the furnace broke, for example, Jake would come into Dad's office and say, "Pastor, I swear that furnace is just plumb come from gether." Well, it makes sense. If, when you fix something, you put it together, then when something breaks, it must have come "from gether"! And so I cannot help but observe that the world is not being put together, whatever Paul or others may claim about the righteous activity of God. But, quite the contrary, the world is coming from gether.

This observation—that the world is falling apart—is, without question, one with which Paul and his Jewish contemporaries would have agreed. What, then, of their affirmation that God is righteous? This question leads us to a second definition of God's righteousness: God's righteousness is God's covenant faithfulness.

LIVING IN RELATIONSHIP

With this second definition, we turn to an understanding of God's righteousness that is related to the conviction that this shalom-making God is a God who has been and is actively involved in the human world. God's goal for the whole world is shalom. The means by which YHWH has chosen to bring shalom to the world is the making of a covenant with a particular group of people. Through this people, YHWH will be known to all the nations.

The first eleven chapters of the book of Genesis tell the story of God's creation of the world and the subsequent disintegration of that creation, especially the human world. But in chapter 12 the narrative takes a new direction. We read in Gen 12:1–3,

Now YHWH said to Abram, "Go from your country and your kindred and your father's house to the land that I will show you. And I will make of you a great nation, and I will bless you, and make your name great, so that you will be a blessing. I will bless those who bless you, and whoever curses you I will curse; and by you all the families of the earth shall bless themselves."

At the close of chapter 11, with the dispersal of the nations at Babel, the world clearly is falling apart. So God begins again, as it were, but this time employs a new strategy in order to recreate the world. God calls a man named Abram, who is later called Abraham, and through him and the nation of his descendants "all the families of the earth shall bless themselves."

God's righteousness now takes on a new dimension. YHWH strikes up a relationship with a specific group of people and through this relationship will bring shalom to the world. God's righteousness is thus expressed in God's covenant faithfulness within a specific commitment to the people called Israel.[1] The identity of Israel is directly related to the covenant God made with them, first with their forefather Abraham and later with all of Israel at Mount Sinai. We read about this commitment between God and Israel in Exodus 19.

On the third new moon after the Israelites had gone out of the land of Egypt, on that very day, they came into the wilderness of Sinai. They had journeyed from Rephidim, entered the wilderness of Sinai, and camped in the wilderness; Israel camped there in front of the mountain. Then Moses went up to God; the LORD called to him from the mountain, saying, "Thus you shall say to the house of Jacob, and tell the Israelites: You have seen what I did to the Egyptians, and how I bore you on eagles' wings and brought you to myself. Now therefore, if you obey my voice and keep my covenant, you shall be my treasured possession out of all the peoples. Indeed, the whole earth is mine, but you shall be for me a priestly kingdom and a holy nation. These are the words that you shall speak to the Israelites."

So Moses came, summoned the elders of the people, and set before them all these words that the LORD had commanded him. The people all answered as one: "Everything that the LORD has spoken we will do." (Exod 19:1–8)

Here we have a "marriage ceremony," where two parties commit themselves one to another: God and Israel exchange vows.

2:2 Find the Vows

Find the vows that Israel and God make in the passage quoted above. What does Israel promise? What does God promise?

Inasmuch as God remains faithful to these "marital" vows, God is righteous. Paul, like any Jew of his day, was fully confident that God is righteous, that God has been faithful to Israel. God has not reneged on the bargain. The Bible refers to this bargain be-

tween God and Israel as a covenant. A covenant is something like a contract, but it is a special kind of contract. We make contracts all the time. Sometimes they are explicit, where each party writes down what he or she will do and each party signs a legal document. Other times they are implicit, where the terms of the contract are not completely spelled out but are nevertheless understood by the two parties. In the quotation from Exodus 19, we see God's explicit commitment: "You shall be for me a priestly kingdom and a holy nation." Israel's specific responsibilities in the contract with God are spelled out in Exodus 20, in what we call the Ten Commandments.

But a covenant is more than a contract. In Exodus 19, before God states the terms of the contract, God first describes to Moses what their history has been: "You have seen what I did to the Egyptians, and how I bore you on eagles' wings and brought you to myself." This contract originated between God and Israel in the context of a prior relationship between the two—God and Israel. The Israelites had been in slavery in Egypt. They cried to God, and God rescued them from that slavery (see Exod 1:14).

2:3 Identifying Contracts

A contract is an agreement between (at least) two people. Some contracts are explicit, formal contracts. These are generally written, signed agreements. Other contracts are implicit contracts, where nothing is written or even spoken but there is an understood agreement between the two parties.

1. Examples of written contracts include a lease or a loan. Can you think of other formal legal contracts where the terms of the agreement are spelled out?
2. An example of an implicit, unwritten contract might include, for instance, the unstated agreement that I as wife do the laundry and you as husband take out the garbage (or vice versa). Friends also have unstated agreements. How would you describe what might be in the "contract" you have with one of your friends? (You might even want to discuss this with your friend!) For example, do you always eat lunch together? Or do you write to one another?

2:4 The Experience of Covenant

The following questions may help you think about the function of contracts within relationships.

1. How is marriage different from living together? What are the advantages and disadvantages of living together? Of marriage?
2. See if you can use the terms contract, relationship, and covenant in describing the difference between marriage and living together.
3. For further thought: Is it possible to have a genuine covenant without a legal (i.e., state-approved) contract? That is, does a covenant require approval by some authoritative body in order to be a covenant? For example, are homosexual "marriages" covenants? Are lifelong friendships covenants? What are the advantages of having a public ceremony of commitment and an official declaration of the commitment (by a priest, rabbi, judge)?

This, then, is what makes a covenant different from, and more than, a contract: A covenant is a contract between two people who are already in a relationship and wish to continue that relationship. Whereas a contract often has a limited term, a covenant implies that this relationship will be a long-term commitment, usually stated in terms of "forever." The function of the contract aspect of a covenant is to allow the relationship to survive over the long term.

Illustration 4
Covenant

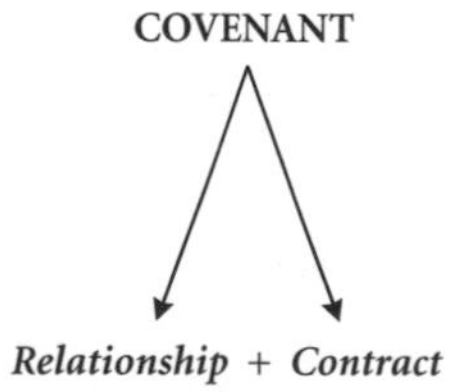

COVENANT

Relationship + Contract

A covenant may be defined as a contract within an ongoing relationship. The purpose of the contract is to nurture and maintain the relationship.

So the covenant between God and Israel is, indeed, very much like a marriage.

On the wedding day, when the bride and the groom say their vows, it is understood that these vows arise out of a relationship that has already been going on for some time. But the vows also point forward. The couple commit themselves to "love, honor, and cherish" and thus to maintain this special relationship "until death do us part." The marriage vows are thus a covenant between the bride and the groom—both the contract and the relationship are essential elements.

God is righteous. That is, God has been faithful both to the contract made with Israel at Sinai and to the relationship between God and Israel, where Israel is "God's chosen people." God has not rejected Israel, nor has God been unfaithful. Thus, the question "Why is the world coming from gether?" cannot be answered, according to Paul or his Jewish contemporaries, by claiming that God is unrighteous. Rather, the answer is that God's people are unrighteous; that is, they have not upheld their end of the covenant. They have broken faith with God. And thus God's shalom-making righteousness has been thwarted.

COVENANT—BROKEN AND RENEWED

What, then, can be done? Is Israel's unrighteousness greater than God's righteousness?[2] Can the covenant, the marriage, between God and Israel be mended? These questions lead us to the third definition of righteousness. If God's righteousness is God's shalom-making activity in the world, then cannot God bring shalom in the marriage between God and Israel? Of course God can! Thus, God's righteousness is the action of God that makes right the relationship between God and humans.

In the Greek language (the language Paul spoke), the notion of righteousness could also be spoken as a verb. In English we don't have a verb form of *righteousness*—only the noun *(righteousness)* and the adjective *(righteous)*. In our English translations of Paul's Greek, when he uses the verb form of *righteous,* the translators use *justify.* Thus, in our English translations we find *righteous, righteousness, justify,* and *justification.* These are very different-looking words in our language. But in Paul's language they were all the same! Study the chart below, where I have listed the Greek words (in English letters) and show their equivalent in English translation:

Illustration 5
"Righteousness" in Greek and English

δικαιοσύνη = righteousness or justification
dikaiosynē

δίκαιος = righteous or just
dikaios

δικαιόω = I justify; I make or declare righteous
dikaioō

δίκη = justice
dikē

A comparison of the Greek words Paul uses related to righteousness with the English translations of those words as found in our English Bibles.

So, in English we say that God is righteous when God justifies (makes righteous) one who has violated the covenant. God's righteousness is God's justification (making righteous) of Israel.

How is such justification possible? The covenant between God and Israel was a covenant between God and a people. But a people is made up of persons. And the violation of the covenant that the people Israel made with God can only occur when real, flesh-and-blood people, when individual Israelites, break the contract with God (remember the Ten Commandments?).

It is not unusual in our human covenants that one member of the covenant will break the contract. In a marriage there are a multitude of ways that the husband or wife can fail to love, honor, and cherish the partner. But if the marriage covenant were completely broken every time the wife or the husband failed to be a good spouse, then the divorce rate would be even higher than it already is! No, most of us know that however painful it may be to experience a specific failure in a marriage, it is possible to put right the marriage (make it righteous, justified) if both the wife and the husband still want the relationship to work out. If the offending spouse returns to the one who has been offended, asks forgiveness, and makes an honest recommitment to the relationship and to the contract (to love, honor, and cherish), the offended spouse may well accept the offender.

When we fail to live up to our relationships, but return and admit that we fouled up, our spouse or our friend or our parent may well justify us—that is, accept us back into the relationship as a full covenant partner.

As in our human relationships we can identify a process we might call the reestablishment of the relationship, so we can see in the Jewish thought of Paul's day a clear process of justification whereby God makes right those

2:5 The Experience of Justification

1. Identify times when you have done something that offended someone with whom you were in relationship. Did you return to the friend or family member? Did he or she accept you? How do you know that you were accepted?
2. Has there ever been a time when you accepted someone who had done something that hurt you? Why did you accept the person? (Or why didn't you?) Describe both your feelings and your thoughts about accepting this person who hurt you.

whose obedience to the covenant has faltered. The process looks like this:

Illustration 6
Process of Justification

Violation of the covenant through transgression of the commandment, which rightly leads to

Guilt on the part of the one who has transgressed, which leads to

Repentance, a "turning away" from the error and back to YHWH, whereupon

Forgiveness is granted by YHWH, and thus the transgressor is

Justified, i.e., restored to the relationship with YHWH and Israel.

Paul's own understanding of the process of justification was significantly different from that reflected in this pattern. But in order to understand this difference (which we will begin to discuss in chapter 5), we must first understand where Paul began. Our purpose now is to understand that Paul and his Jewish contemporaries did agree that one's justification does not depend upon human perfection; they agreed that God is able to re-establish the relationship with those who have strayed.

Thus, we can say that *to be justified* is somewhat synonymous with *to be accepted.* But it is important to recognize that such ac-

2:6 A Healthy Relationship

The essential difference between our common understanding of righteousness and Paul's understanding is that we frequently think of righteousness as a description of a good individual while, for Paul, righteousness is ultimately a description of a healthy relationship. Since righteousness is a covenantal term, there must be, in order for a person to be righteous, an other to be in right relationship with. One cannot be righteous just by virtue of doing right things.

I may be righteous in relation to some people and unrighteous in relation to others. I may, in fact, do some wrong things in a relationship, but as long as I am honestly seeking to remain in the relationship (through repentance and forgiveness, if necessary), I may still be described as striving for righteousness.

See if you can think of relationships where you have known righteousness, where you have been aware of being in right relationship. How did/does it feel to be in a healthy relationship?

Whenever you hear the term righteousness, identify the term with the experience of being in right relationship with an other. Eventually you may begin to "forget" the (mistaken) conception of righteousness as being the performance of right acts and learn (from Paul and Judaism) that righteousness is a measurement of relational wholeness rather than of individual morality.

ceptance is not necessarily an easy forgiveness. It is a tough love: In order for Israel, for an Israelite, to be accepted back into the covenant relationship, each must first acknowledge having in fact broken the contract. There is always an element of judgment in justification. If I have offended my spouse or my parent or my friend, I must admit that I have broken the contract, that I have messed up, and I must be willing to change, to turn around. Thus, in the Hebrew Bible (as well as in the Greek world), the word *righteousness* (or *justification*) is frequently found in legal contexts. We stand before a court of law, acknowledging that we have violated the contract, and God, who is a merciful and gracious judge, acquits us and restores us to relationship within the covenant.[3] If, however, we are unwilling to stand under the judgment, if either we are unwilling to say that we have violated the contract or we don't care that we have violated the covenant, then no justification will be granted and divorce is the only option. Justification depends, then, not just on God's mercy but also on our willingness to continue this marriage relationship, this covenant with God.

CONCLUSION

God is righteous, and God's righteousness is expressed in relation to the cosmos, in relation to the nation Israel, and in relation to individuals within Israel. Because God is righteous, God will justify those who fail to live within the relationship. God will acquit them and accept them back into the covenant if they return to God. This scenario assumes, of course, that individual Israelites want to remain in the relationship with God. If both the contract and the relationship are shattered, then the covenant is indeed broken. Justification (making righteous) is possible between God and Israel only as long as Israel wants a healthy relationship with this God, with YHWH. In the next chapter we will discover how Israel can remain within a relationship with YHWH.

READING CHECK

☑ What are the three definitions of righteousness given in this chapter?

☑ There is a progression in the discussion of these three aspects of righteousness—from a broad definition of righteousness (cosmic), to a narrower definition (national), to a very narrow definition (individual). Identify the definitions you have given for question 1, above, by placing a C by the "cosmic definition," an N by the "national definition," and an I by the "individual definition."

☑ What is the relationship between the words righteousness and justification?

☑ How is God's relationship with Israel like a marriage? What is the technical biblical term for this kind of relationship?

☑ How does God prevent a "divorce" from happening in God's relationship to Israel? How does Israel prevent a "divorce" from happening in Israel's relationship to God?

*T*his chapter describes a Jewish view of the law. In his own thought, Paul presupposes this understanding of the law. As you will see in part 2, however, Paul's views on the law are much more complex than what is represented here.

In this chapter you will discover that obeying the law leads to joy because obedience to the law is the means to shalom. Three qualifying statements will be added to the statement "Obedience to the law is the means to shalom." Identify these three qualifiers clearly in the margins of the text. When you are through reading this chapter, you should be able to articulate why and how obedience to the law can be a joyous and freeing life.

3

Law

God's Gracious Gift

We often perceive law as a necessary evil. People often define freedom as "being able to do what I want when I want." Laws are unfortunate but necessary restrictions on our freedom, so that "my" freedom does not violate "your" freedom. We tend to focus more on our rights than on our responsibility. But to Paul and the Jews, the law[1] was something for which they were grateful. For instance, read Psalm 19 for a hymn celebrating the law. Obedience to the law was understood to be a joy, certainly not a necessary

---

3:1 A Selection from Psalm 19

The fear of the LORD is clean, enduring for ever;
the ordinances of the LORD are true, and righteous altogether.
More to be desired are they than gold, even much fine gold;
sweeter also than honey and drippings of the honeycomb.
Moreover, by them is thy servant warned;
in keeping them there is great reward.
But who can discern his errors?
Clear thou me from hidden faults.
Keep back thy servant also from presumptuous sins; let them not have dominion over me!
Then I shall be blameless, and innocent of great transgression.
Let the words of my mouth and the meditation of my heart be acceptable in thy sight,
O LORD, my rock and my redeemer. (RSV)

evil. Thus, as with *righteousness,* you will need to remember that *law* is a term with positive, rather than negative, connotations.

THE LAW AS GUIDANCE

God's goal for the cosmos is shalom. The primary means by which God has chosen to accomplish this goal is the establishment of a special covenant with the people Israel. Through this covenant God will bless all the nations of the world and will thus bring the peace God has always intended for humanity. God has been and is faithful to this covenant; God is righteous. It is incumbent upon Israel, then, to do its part by being faithful to its covenant with God, so that God's purposes might be fully accomplished in the world.

But how can Israel know whether it is faithful to the covenant? How can the people of Israel be sure that they are being faithful partners with God in bringing peace to their world? God knows the part that God must play in this covenant; that is, God knows God's own contractual responsibilities in the relationship with Israel. Israel, however, needs God's guidance in order to know what part to play, in order to know what its contractual responsibilities in the covenant are. The law provides just such guidance for Israel. The law is God's gracious gift to Israel, explaining what its part in covenant faithfulness is.

The logic of the law is very simple. Indeed, it is something that we experience in many areas of our own lives. For example,

students enter into a covenant of sorts with the college or the university that they attend.[2] We enroll in an institution of higher learning in order to get an education. How do we know if we have received an education after the four years we spend in college? Do we receive an education just by virtue of establishing a relationship with the institution—whether through attendance or through money? Probably not. The institution must do its part—by providing a strong curriculum and a good faculty and adequate facilities and resources for study. But even if the institution does its part, we will surely not get an education unless we do our part as students. But what is our part? The college or university has (we trust) thought much about this question. The result of this thought can be found in the college catalogue. A college catalogue is, for the student, the law in relation to the goal of arriving at a college education. Thus, it is important to read the catalogue carefully; it is a contract between the student and the school. If the student fulfills all the requirements as stated in that catalogue (law), he or she will arrive at the hoped-for destination—not simply graduation but an education.

This phenomenon of law as guidance is also found in specific courses. When you register for a course, you form a covenant with the professor. Even if you have never stated it explicitly, you know when a professor is unfaithful to this covenant; that is, you know when the professor is unrighteous. If she fails to show up for class, or if

---

3:2 Examples of the Law as Guidance

Can you suggest other examples of how law (or rules) serves as guidance? For instance, describe how having a clearly written job description can help you do your job better. What are some other examples that you can think of?

he teaches you calculus when you enrolled in a class on Chinese history, then the professor has been unfaithful to the covenant. Assuming for the moment, however, that your professor is faithful to the covenant, what must you as students do to be faithful? How can you do your part in order to arrive at the common goal—an education in the particular topic of this course? Inevitably, when I ask my students this question, I get the response, "Do the work!" Yes, indeed. Do the work. But what is the work? The answer to this question is found on your course syllabus under the heading "Requirements." These requirements for the course are the law for you in your quest of learning the material for this course. Now admittedly, sometimes a professor does not do an adequate job in drawing up the requirements for the course. But imagine for a moment (if this isn't stretching the imagination too far!) that the professor is an extremely wise, greatly experienced educator and that such a professor has carefully and thoughtfully crafted for you a syllabus that will ensure, if you follow it faithfully, that you will, indeed, receive a full and exciting education in the topic at hand. In this case, the syllabus is the professor's gracious gift to you as students. It provides a sure way for you to enter fully into the educational venture that is your heart's goal. Similarly, then, the law is God's gracious gift of a syllabus to Israel.

THE LAW AS THE WAY OF SALVATION

The Israelites want to be in covenantal relationship with this God. YHWH has saved them from slavery and sustained them throughout the centuries. They know that their relationship with YHWH means life for them. And they know that this God is "a gracious God and merciful, slow to anger, and abounding in steadfast love."[3] The law provides for the Israelites, for the Jewish people, the way to be faithful in their relationship with this shalom-making God. The law is the way to shalom, both for Israel and for the world.

Thus, obedience to the law is the means to shalom. This statement sounds simple, but it is not. Let me clarify this simple statement by making it more complex.

The Law Brings Freedom

First, the phrase *obedience to the law* is not likely to arouse joy or excitement in us. Obeying the law, any law, sounds more like drudgery and boredom to many of us. It perhaps sounds like confinement, like a sort of slavery. But Israel understands this obedience as being an exciting, joyous way of life. Obeying the law brings true freedom. Remember that Israel wants to be in right relationship with this shalom-making God; this is the people of Israel's deepest, most heart-

---

3:3 The Law as Gracious Gift

On occasion I have written a course syllabus where I do not specify exactly what I want the students to do. That is, I give the students several suggestions but leave it up to them to "contract" with me exactly how they want to fulfill the requirements for the course.

1. What are the advantages and disadvantages of this system for the student?
2. Explain, then, how the "law" (whether it be given by your professor or an institution or your parents) can be understood to be a "gracious gift."

felt goal. If the law is the way to attain their deepest desire, then fulfilling this law will bring them great joy.

Imagine that your deepest desire is to be a professional dancer, not because you want fame and fortune particularly but simply because you love to dance. Now, if this is truly your goal, then you know that you must practice dancing. You must take lessons. You must spend hours every day for years and years doing nothing but dancing. This is the "law" of becoming a professional dancer. Is it a burden? Yes, sometimes, because you must forego other desirable activities. Is it drudgery? Yes, sometimes, because dancing is exhausting and you will have to spend hours practicing repetitive movements. Is it a joy? Absolutely! Because there is nothing in this world that you would rather be doing than dancing. It is in dancing that you know real freedom in this life. It is in dancing that you are in touch with all that is truly alive. And it is only in dancing daily that you will ever hope to be free to be a professional dancer.

So it is, for Israelites, with obedience to the law. They know from their own experience that being in right relationship with YHWH is joy. They experienced despair; they were enslaved in Egypt. Pharaoh had his own law, and it was an oppressive law, a law that was forced upon them. Pharoah's law was not a covenantal law. It was simply the expression of Pharoah's own will. The Hebrew people had no choice in the matter.

But the law of YHWH was a different kind of law altogether. For YHWH met the people of Israel at Sinai. This God who had delivered them, this God who had already saved them, now approached them with the offer of a covenant relationship. Do you, Israel, choose to enter into covenantal relationship with this God? And Israel said, "Yes, everything that YHWH has spoken we will do!" (Exod 19:8). And Israel continued to affirm this commitment. Read Joshua 24 for an important renewal ceremony between God and Israel. Again and again, Israel has chosen to serve God and obey God's gracious law. This law, then, is not oppressive. It is not the law of a dictator. Rather, this law provides the way to be in a joyous relationship with a loving and gracious God who intends to bring shalom to the entire cosmos. If obeying the law is the way to attain this joy and this shalom, and if obeying the law is itself the experience of this joy and shalom, then obedience to the law is joy and peace. The people of Israel long for the shalom of God in their own history. It gives meaning to all of life.

Shalom Is Not a Reward

Second, obedience to the law is the means to shalom, but shalom is not a reward for obedience. Here we meet head-on one of the most frequent misunderstandings about the law. If it is true that the law is the means to shalom, then one might argue that one can attain shalom simply by keeping the law. It is critical that we understand this misinterpretation of the law. Perhaps it will be clearer to use the language of the church: Salvation

3:4 The Joy of Obedience

Does the illustration of the dancer make sense to you? What is it that you most want to do or be in this life? (It will help if you choose some specific activity, rather than a broad "what I want out of life.") What must you do in order to "practice" this? What is the "law" that you will need to obey in order to be what you want to be? And (this part is important) will you enjoy obeying that law?

is not a reward for obedience. The longing for shalom can also be described as the longing for salvation. The argument that one can attain salvation by keeping the law leads to a faulty conclusion; it betrays a misunderstanding of the relationship between law and salvation. The relationship of law to salvation is not a mathematical relationship of "if A, then B": If X keeps the law, then X will be saved. Rather, keeping the law is a description of what is essential for shalom's existence.

The law enables Israel to maintain a righteous relationship with God. The goal of this righteous relationship is shalom, both for Israel and for the world. The problem with the "if A, then B" formula is that it implies that Israel's obedience will necessarily bring about shalom. In philosophical terms, this would be equivalent to saying that Israel's obedience to the law is both a necessary and a sufficient condition for shalom. But such an assertion ignores the middle term of righteousness. Law enables righteousness in the relationship with God. And it is this relationship that will eventually produce shalom in God's world. Israel's obedience will not bring shalom; only God can do that. But God has chosen to bring this shalom through God's engagement with the people Israel. Shalom will be the fruit of this righteous relationship.

When we leave out the crucial middle term of righteousness, we misunderstand the function of the law. It is righteousness, not the law, that bears the fruit of shalom. We might think of obedience as the activity of watering the tree of righteousness. One cannot simply pour water on the ground and assume that fruit will appear! No, one has to water the roots of the tree. It is the tree that bears the fruit, not the water. But without the water, the tree will die and there will be no fruit.

Thus, the law is always focused upon righteousness. Its sole purpose is to further Israel's relationship with God. The law does not, and cannot, exist by itself, apart from this relationship. God does not go around dropping fruit on Israel simply because Israel waters the ground: shalom is not a reward for obedience. No, obedience nurtures a loving relationship, a relationship with this shalom-making God.

Obeying Together

Third, the shalom that the law brings is corporate and cosmic. In today's world, we often think of shalom in terms of the individual, as personal salvation. This is perhaps due to the influence of Christianity in the Western world.[4] But the salvation for which Israel longs is primarily the salvation of Israel as a nation, and through Israel the world itself will know the shalom/salvation of YHWH. Thus, it is important, even crucial, that all of Israel obey the law. It would not do for an individual Jew to be concerned only about his

---

3:5 Obeying the Law of Relationships

1. Is friendship the reward that one earns by virtue of having "done the right things" in order to be a friend? Why or why not?
2. What does it take to have a good friendship? What is the "law of friendship"? What does friendship "produce"? Can you draw a picture of friendship as a tree? Label the tree "friendship." Now, what is the fruit of that tree? How does one water a friendship?

or her adherence to the law. In Genesis, Cain asked God, "Am I my brother's keeper?" The Jews would answer this question with a resounding "Yes!" To love God is to love the neighbor. Love of neighbor is not just another law but, rather, a summary of the law. One loves one's neighbor as a means of fulfilling the law, not just for one's own righteousness but to enable one's neighbor to be free to fulfill the law as well.

Perhaps we know this corporate dynamic of the law best in the world of team sports. You cannot have a winning team just because everyone on the team follows the rules. They must follow them together, as a unit. And they must do so in creative ways, not just as a matter of rote. Similarly, an orchestra must play the score together. Anyone who has heard a beginning band struggle to play a song knows how difficult it can be for everyone to play the score well. But even if every student in the band plays every note with precision, the result is not necessarily musical. Each member, of a team or of an orchestra, must play with a constant awareness of every other member of the team or orchestra. The goal of winning the game or playing the music demands that everyone follow the rules together. Obedience to the law (to the rules, to the musical score) cannot be an individual affair. To be sure, every individual must attend to the rules or the score. It is not that some great corporate

spirit simply takes over and makes a winning team or a great orchestra; each member must do her or his part, and do it well. But the individual members must always perceive themselves as a part of a greater whole. Otherwise, even their individual effort will fail.

Similarly, obedience to the law is a joint affair; it is something we do together. Indeed, it cannot be done alone. Israel obeys the law together for Israel's salvation, and for the salvation of the world.

CONCLUSION

Thus, the simple statement, obedience to the law is the means to shalom, needs some additional qualifiers. Obedience to the law is the joyous journey that a person makes on the way to full participation in corporate and cosmic salvation. Through the law Israel knows the way of life, the way of righteousness, the way of shalom. Through the law Israel participates with God in God's act of bringing shalom to the whole world. Thus, obedience to the law is joy and peace and freedom.

Although we are leaving here our discussion of the term *law,* we're not through with law yet. What has been said so far about law can be described as Paul's starting point. We will see in part 2 that Paul has some other, startling ideas about the law.

3:6 Obeying the Law Together

Can you think of other illustrations where "joint obedience" is essential in order for success to occur? In what areas is your own success necessarily limited because the others involved are not "obedient," are not committed to the task? Do you think that it helps your success at work or as a student when others around you share your desire for the success of the work?

READING CHECK

☑ How is the law like a syllabus?

☑ What are the three qualifying statements that need to be added to the simple statement "Obedience to the law is the means to salvation"?

☑ What new ideas about the law did you learn from reading this chapter?

☑ Describe how obedience to the law can lead a person to a joyous and freeing life.

part one

Summary and Review

SUMMARY

The last three chapters have provided a basic introduction into the foundations of Paul's thought. Paul was a Jew, and as such he shared with others in the Jewish community a fundamental belief that the *God of Israel* was committed to bringing *shalom* to the universe. The Jewish community was central to God's plan; they were God's *covenant* partners in this plan. That is, inasmuch as Israel (the Jewish community) was faithful to the covenant with God, it shared in God's *righteousness*. Through obedience to the *law* Israel maintained the covenant relationship with God and participated in God's righteous activity in this world.

The italicized words in the previous paragraph identify key terms of Paul's thought: *God of Israel, shalom, covenant, righteousness*, and *law*. All of these terms derive from Paul's Jewish community and this community's understanding of human life and history. Jews' understanding of these matters was, in significant respects, different from the understanding of their Greco-Roman neighbors. Most notable for our purposes, the Jewish understanding of the goal of human life was communal and historical. Human aspirations were directly linked with the dream of God to bring shalom to the whole world. Individual human happiness or serenity was not the highest goal. Rather, a person's participation in God's cosmic purposes was central. Thus, it was not human mastery of one's own life that was most important. Only through obedience to this gracious God and participation in God's righteousness could a person know ultimate fulfillment.

This basic understanding of human life and purpose lay at the very heart of Paul's thinking. Even after his encounter with Christ (which we will explore in part 3), these central concepts of righteousness, shalom, covenant, and law continued to be central to his understanding of human life. He never forsook this basic Jewish commitment. Still, Paul's encounter with Christ altered his understanding of his commitment, and thus of these key terms, in crucial ways. In the next three chapters (part 2) we will look at how Paul's understanding of humanity affected his conception of the law. It is very important, therefore, that the first three chapters be seen as provisional, not because they have articulated a view of righteousness or law that Paul leaves behind once he encounters Christ but, rather, because Paul extends and elaborates—sometimes in startling ways—these foundational concepts. The fundamental contours of these key terms—*righteousness* and *law*—are still determinative in his later thought.

Thus, it is crucial to grasp the centrality of Paul's Jewish commitments at the outset of this study. Even after he becomes the Apostle to the Gentiles, Paul himself continues to be committed to his Jewish heritage. His conception of the deep agony of sin as an inability to attain a righteous relationship (see chapter 5) depends upon an appreciation of the supreme value of righteousness and the gift of the law as understood within the Jewish community. Similarly, in order to understand why Paul believed Christ was the revelation of God's righteousness, it is crucial to know what righteousness was and why humans longed to know God's righteousness.

At the end of each of the following two parts, it will be helpful for you to return to these foundational chapters and ask how Paul's teaching on sin and death, or on Christ, both depends upon these concepts of righteousness and law and elaborates these concepts in new ways.

REVIEW

A. Terms and Concepts

1. Diaspora
2. monotheist
3. YHWH
4. eschatology
5. promise-fulfillment eschatology
6. prophetic eschatology
7. apocalyptic eschatology
8. Yavneh
9. the saints
10. Moses
11. righteousness
12. shalom
13. covenant
14. Abraham
15. Ten Commandments
16. justification
17. process of justification
18. Torah
19. law
20. obedience

B. Making Connections

The notions of shalom, righteousness, and law can be understood analogously as dream, desire, and discipline. God's dream is shalom. God's active desire for this dream is righteousness. And law is the discipline of living toward that dream, living out the active desire. God, of course, does not need to articulate a law for God's own righteous pursuit of shalom. But Israel has committed itself to be God's covenant partner in pursuing shalom for this world. Thus, from the human standpoint, Israel shares God's dream (shalom) and God's active desire (righteousness). The law guides Israel in the discipline of living out this dream.

In order to grasp the internal dynamics of shalom, righteousness, and law, it might help you to think of an analogous set of "dream . . . desire . . . discipline." Either through writing in a journal or through composing a short essay, reflect on the following questions:

1. What is your life dream? Describe it in as much detail as you can. Dream big. It can be anything you dream of—world peace, financial security for your family, a role on Broadway, election to national office, writing the great American novel, raising a family. Why is this your dream? What are your feelings about this dream (your analogous term for *shalom*)?

2. What are some indications that you are already engaged in active pursuit of this dream? What are you doing now that gives expression to the larger dream or desire that you have for your life (your analogous term for *righteousness*)?

3. What are your plans for pursuing this dream? How do you (or will you need to) discipline yourself—your time, your money, your desires, your relationships— in order to make this dream become a reality? Be as specific as you can. Outline an ideal day in pursuit of this dream. What would you do? What would you not do? How do you feel about engaging in these disciplines (your analogous term for *law*)?

4. Israel's dream, desire, and discipline were not, of course, simply an individual matter. Thus, in order to understand more of the communal dimensions of these concepts, imagine how your dream might be a communal matter. What differences would it make in your dream, desire, and discipline if you were to share these with someone else—with a friend, a spouse, or a community? How would (or does) it feel to commit yourself to a dream with someone else and to share the discipline of realizing that dream? In what ways does such dream sharing enhance the dream, desire, and discipline? In what ways does it feel restrictive?

5. Finally, interview a good friend or family member and ask them this same set of questions. Or discuss these questions in a small group of interested friends. What do you learn from this interview or discussion?

Paul's Greco-Roman Milieu

An Enslaved Humanity

*T*he previous three chapters describe some aspects of the Jewish heritage that Paul shared with other Jews of his day. The stories and thought of Israel provided Paul with the primary language and symbols for his "map making." The map that Paul draws, however, is also influenced by the topography of the Greco-Roman context in which he lived and thought. It is the goal of this chapter to delineate in broad strokes some of the relevant intellectual contours of this context. At the end of the chapter you should be able to identify at least three intellectual concerns that Paul shared with some of the non-Jewish thinkers in the Greco-Roman world.

4

Paul among the Gentiles

"No Distinction between Jew and Greek"

Paul was a Jewish missionary among the Gentiles. He worked actively and tirelessly to convince other people (both Jews and Gentiles) that his vision of life was worthy of consideration. Such missionary work was not unusual activity in the Greco-Roman world of Paul's time. Today we associate the word *missionary* with a religious vocation: A missionary attempts to convert someone to another religion. In Paul's day, however, philosophers often undertook efforts at conversion. A philosophy is, after all, a vision of life. And a philosopher in the Greco-Roman world frequently saw it as part of his duty to proclaim his philosophy publicly so that other people might adopt a superior vision of life.

Some of the Gentiles in the cities where Paul traveled might well have taken him for a philosopher. Certainly many of his practices and some of the topics of interest to him would have made him look like a Greco-Roman philosopher.[1] Paul, like the philosophers, was interested in human identity and society. Like other thinkers of his day, he could not help but observe that something in human society had gone terribly wrong. And like the philosophers, Paul was convinced that the problem with human society lay in the individual's failure to perceive the world accurately.

In the last three chapters we became acquainted with the traditions that Paul had received from his Jewish training. Now it is time to explore how Paul used the language of his tradition in order to make sense of his Greco-Roman context. In this chapter we will look at three intellectual problems with which both Paul and the philosophers wrestled as they struggled to articulate their different visions for human life.

HUMAN IDENTITY IN SOCIETY

Ancient Israel was a tribal society. Identity was determined by one's place and role

4:1 The Source of Our Identity

1. Think about how your own identity is related to your social context. On a scale of 1 to 5 (1 = not at all; 5 = very much) how would you answer the following questions?

   To what extent—

   —do you draw your understanding of yourself from where you grew up?

       1   2   3   4   5

   —do you think that you would have the same personality no matter where you lived?

       1   2   3   4   5

   —do you consider yourself a "citizen of the universe"?

       1   2   3   4   5

2. Write a short paragraph explaining why you answered these questions the way you did.

in the tribe. But the Israel of Paul's day lived in a very different world from the one in which its ancestors lived. Since at least the time of Alexander the Great (died 323 B.C.E.), the peoples who lived in the areas around the Mediterranean Sea had begun to mingle with one another. The old tribal societies, Israelite and Greek alike, began to break down.

The Greek philosophers had occasion to think much about the various ethnic peoples and their diverse customs. How can a person know who he or she is when the tribal society breaks down, when there is no clear place within a specific tribe? Whose customs and laws are best—those of Egypt? Greece? Rome? Judea? Does one's ethnic identity or political citizenship determine how one should act? With the world shifting and mixing so dramatically, how can a person know who he or she is?

The Greek philosopher Diogenes (born fourth century B.C.E.) declared, "I am a citizen of the world."[2] One's identity, the philosophers insisted, was determined by one's character and virtue. No particular ethnic membership or political citizenship was necessary for personal identity. Rather, there was a universal citizenship available to all. The philosophies that emerged from this insight of Diogenes thus posed a new understanding of the relationship between the individual and society. In ancient tribal societies the individual was defined almost solely in relation to the local community. Your identity was your role in society. Your family, your occupation, your specific social status in the community—all these things constituted your identity. But determining an identity based on citizenship in a universal community was a quite different task from defining oneself based on a specific and inherited role in a particular community. Inevitably, then, the individual came to acquire more importance in these later philosophies, and much of this philosophical thought dealt with how the individual could be virtuous in relation to the universe rather than in relation to a specific community and its peculiar laws.

Paul's writings show that Paul, too, was interested in, and concerned about, the relationship between individuals and society. In particular, he was concerned to demonstrate that the one true God, the God of Israel, was a universal God. As he says to the Romans,

> Is God the God of Jews only? Is he not the God of Gentiles also? Yes, of Gentiles also, since God is one. (Rom 3:29)

This God, who traveled alongside Israel in the past centuries, is not, according to Paul, an ethnic or local God. The Jews may well have lived in local and enclosed communities for centuries. But their God was a universal God who transcended the particularities of Jewish ethnicity.

Unlike the philosophers, however, Paul did not propose a straightforward universal citizenship. Membership in the covenantal community was universally available; that is, it was available to all. But membership in this community demanded faith in the one true God, the God of Israel. The community of God's people, Jews and Gentiles who trusted the revelation of God, was not cosmopolitan. In Paul's view, the "saints" were neither Jew nor Gentile (Gal 3:28) but were nevertheless individual members of the particular community that had covenanted with YHWH to bring shalom to the cosmos.

One of the consequences of Paul's conviction that membership in the covenantal community was universally available is that he leveled the playing field, so to speak, between Jews and Gentiles. In his Letter to the Romans Paul makes clear that, in his judgment, both Jews and Gentiles have "fallen short of the glory of God" (Rom 3:23). Citing passages from his own tradition (see sidebar 4:2), Paul argues,

> What then? Are we Jews any better off [than the Gentiles]? No, not at all; for I have already charged that all, both Jews and Greeks, are under the power of sin. (Rom 3:9)

4:2 A Selection from Psalm 53

The fool says in his heart, "There is no God."
    They are corrupt, doing abominable iniquity;
    there is none that does good.
God looks down from heaven upon humanity
    to see if there are any that are wise, that
    seek after God.
They have all fallen away; they are all alike
    depraved;
    there is none that does good, no, not one.

The phrases "fallen short of the glory of God" and "under the power of sin" in the above citations from Romans take us into new territory in our study. The concept of sin will occupy us throughout part 2. And although Paul's Jewish tradition spoke much about sin and forgiveness, the Greco-Roman philosophers spoke of the frailty and failure of human life in ways that sound very much like Paul.

THE FRAILTY AND FAILURE OF HUMAN LIFE

We often identify notions of sin solely with religious sensibilities. To some degree, this perception is correct, at least for the language of Paul. The philosophers do use the Greek word *hamartia*, but they use it differently than does Paul or his religious family. For Paul and the Jews, sin was a serious dishonor that ruptured the relationship between God and God's people whereas, for the philosophers (as for many of us), a sin was simply an unfortunate mistake or lapse in judgment. But a comparison of how Paul used the word *hamartia* ("sin") with how the philosophers used the same word ("mistake") does not tell the full story, for the philosophers and Paul did share a common conviction that human life was frail and difficult. This frailty, which Paul included in his notion of sin, the philosophers frequently referred to as a "disease."[3]

Listen to an Epicurean philosopher describe the sickness of humanity:

> If only human beings, just as they seem to feel a weight in their minds that wears them out with its heaviness, could also grasp the causes of this [anguish] and know from what origin such a great mountain of ill stands on their chest, they would hardly lead their lives as we now often see them do, ignorant of what they really want, and always seeking a change of place as if they could put down their burden. Here's a man who often goes outside, leaving his house, because he's tired of being home. Just as suddenly he turns back, since he feels no better outdoors. He rushes off in haste to his country house, bringing his slaves, as if the house were burning down and he had to bring help; he turns back again, as soon as he touches the threshold; or heavy, he seeks forgetfulness in sleep; or, full of haste, he charges back to the city. Thus each person flees himself. But in spite of all his efforts he clings to that self, which we know he never can succeed in escaping, and hates it—all because he is sick and does not know the cause of his sickness.[4]

Certainly not much seems to have changed in the last twenty centuries. How many of our hectic days does this philosopher describe! Running from one thing to another and back again, unable to rest easy with ourselves. The many books on the self-help shelves in bookstores would agree that "each person flees himself . . . all because he is sick and does not know the cause of his sickness."

Paul, as well as other Jews, claimed to know the cause of this human sickness:

> Therefore as sin came into the world through one man and death through sin, so death spread to all because all have sinned. (Rom 5:12)

Because the first human, Adam, sinned, so have we all. Paul was not alone in this understanding of the universal nature of human frailty. Another Jewish text puts it this way:

> For though Adam first sinned and brought untimely death upon all, yet all those who were born from him each one of them has prepared for his own soul torment to come, and again each one of them has chosen for himself glories to come. . . . Adam is therefore not the cause, save only of his own soul, but *each of us has been the Adam of his own soul.* (*2 Bar.* 54:15, 19; emphasis added[5])

Several centuries after Paul, this view of human nature, that "all have sinned," was developed into the doctrine called "original sin";[6] it is rejected by many people because of its apparently negative and defeatist view of human beings. It also seems downright unfair! Why should I be charged with sin simply because Adam screwed up?

In Paul's world, however, this view was neither unfair nor defeatist. He (and *2 Baruch*)

4:3 Because Adam Sinned

1. Have you heard of "original sin"? What does this term mean to you?
2. To what degree, do you think, people's errors are their own fault?
3. Do you think that social context, education, or other external circumstances sometimes contribute to people's failure to live happily or lawfully?
4. Write a short paragraph describing your present understanding of the relationship between individual responsibility and social circumstances and influences.

used the figure of Adam from his Jewish tradition in order to illustrate something important about our human frailty. Our failings are not simply individual failures. Our very socialization sets us up to fail. Perhaps it will help to hear it from a philosopher without the religious connotations of sin getting in the way. Here is a Greek inscription, from the second century C.E., that was recently unearthed in Asia Minor:

> If it was one only, or two or three or four or five or six or however many more than that you want, O human being, but not a very large number, who were in a wretched condition, then calling them one by one. . . . [Here there is a gap in the inscription.] But since, as I said before, most people are sick all together, as in the plague, of false opinion concerning things, and since they are becoming more numerous—for on account of their reciprocal emulation they get the disease from one another like sheep—in addition to the fact that it is *philanthropon* to help strangers who pass by the way—since, then, the aid of this piece of writing goes out to many, I have decided, using this stoa, to put out in public for all the drugs that will save them.[7]

In the language of this inscription, humans have contracted a plague of wretchedness. In the language of Paul and *2 Baruch,* humans have been infected by the sin of Adam. This infection has occurred because "of their reciprocal emulation"—that is, they copy each other. And thus "they get the disease from one another like sheep." The point of Paul's description of the effect of Adam's sin is the same as that of this inscription: Human misery is caused as much by our social involvement as it is by our individual rebellions.

The specific cause of human misery is also indicated by the inscription above: "Most people are sick all together . . . of false opinion concerning things." The philosophers agreed on this: the disease of humanity is a disease of the mind. And here again we see that Paul and the philosophers have some ideas in common.

A DISEASE OF THE MIND

In Romans 1, after a long description of the sinfulness of humanity, Paul declares,

> And since they did not see fit to acknowledge God, God gave them up to a base mind and to improper conduct. They were filled with all manner of wickedness, evil, covetousness, malice. Full of envy, murder, strife, deceit, malignity, they are gossips, slanderers, haters of God, insolent, haughty, boastful, inventors of evil, disobedient to parents, foolish, faithless, heartless, ruthless. Though they know God's decree that those who do such things deserve to die, they not only do them but approve those who practice them. (Rom 1:28–32)

Those who have rejected God have been given up to a "base mind," that is, they cannot think straight. Thus, Paul says to those believers who wish to live in God's world,

> Do not be conformed to this world, but be transformed by the renewal of your mind, that you may prove what is the will of God, what is good and acceptable and perfect. (Rom 12:2)

Paul believes that apart from God humans are unable to think clearly or correctly. The mind is not only the locus of the human disease of sin; as we shall see, the intellect also plays a key role in Paul's vision for a renewed humanity.

In this emphasis on the importance of the intellect and human rationality, Paul reflects again an understanding in common with the philosophers of the first century.[8] One of the central claims of the philosophers was that humans fall into misery because they misunderstand and misperceive their situation. A quote from a Stoic of Paul's day can illustrate.

> Bring whatever you will and I will turn it into a good. Bring disease, bring death, bring poverty, reviling, peril of life in court. . . . Everything that you give I will turn into something blessed, productive of happiness, august, enviable.
>
> Not so you; but [you say] "Watch out that you don't get ill; it's bad." Just as if someone said, "Watch out that you never get the impression that three are four; it's bad." Man, how do you mean "bad"? *If I get the right idea of it, how is it going to hurt me any more?* Will it not rather even do me good? If, then, I get the right idea about poverty, or disease, or not holding office, am I not satisfied? Will they not be helpful to me?[9]

This passage from the Stoic philosopher Epictetus has always amazed me. Bring on disease, death, poverty! Not something that you'll be likely to catch me saying. What an amazing confidence Epictetus had, that he was able to believe that he could turn any trial into something that produced happiness. The key to his confidence lies in the highlighted sentence: "If I get the right idea of [anything], how is it going to hurt me . . . ?" That is, our miseries are caused by our failure to perceive the real nature of things and of ourselves. Today we might talk about the need "to get your head straight." It may be that someday, when you have difficulties in your personal life, you will choose to go to a therapist for help. The therapist will not, of course, change any of the concrete circumstances of your life. But that therapist will help you see the circumstances of your life from a new and healthier perspective. Successful therapy might not lead you to say, "Bring on disease, death, poverty!" but it can help you to cope with such traumas by learning to think about yourself and your life in new ways.

Since, according to the philosophers, the misperception of reality causes the problems that humans face, the goal of philosophy in Paul's day was somewhat like that of therapists today.[10] The philosopher sought to retrain the mind of the student, to teach the student to see things in a new way:

> Right from the start, get into the habit of saying to every harsh appearance, "You are an appearance, and not the only way of seeing the thing that appears." Then examine it and test it by the yardsticks you have.[11]

In short, things are not always as they seem, and it is philosophy's job to train us to see rightly, to perceive the true reality of the world and of ourselves.

Illustration 7
The Play of Perception

Can you perceive both ways of seeing the picture at the same time? Or can you only see either the young girl or the old woman at a given moment?

CONCLUSION

If it is the philosopher's job to help us perceive reality, then it is no wonder that the philosophers of Paul's day were missionaries. Each philosophical school had its own vision of reality. And most philosophical schools felt a duty to proclaim their understanding of reality to an ailing humanity. Paul, too, was a missionary who proclaimed his own understanding of reality to an ailing humanity. While Paul's thinking and practice reflect his own engagement in the general intellectual climate of the Greco-Roman world, the overwhelming influence of Paul's Jewish heritage affected both the vocabulary and the contours of his philosophical mission.

Most important, Paul's view of YHWH as an active agent in the history of Israel defined Paul's vision. Human misperception was the result, in Paul's view, of the mighty evil forces that are depicted in apocalyptic eschatology. These forces had seduced humanity away from God and had perverted human thinking. Paul certainly felt that it was his responsibility to proclaim to the masses his vision of God's reality; yet Paul was convinced that something more than intellectual training was needed in order to correct human misperception—the revelation of God in Christ would be necessary for that. It was, in fact, this revelation of God that enabled Paul to see sin for what it was: a deadly misperception of God, of world, and of self. In the next two chapters we will explore the damning implications of sin and how it leads to death.

READING CHECK:

☑ What is a difference between Diogenes' view of a universal community and Paul's view?

☑ Why do Paul and 2 Baruch say that Adam's sin has infected us today?

☑ Why do Paul and the philosophers place so much emphasis on the mind in their efforts to understand human misery?

☑ Name three intellectual concerns that Paul shared with some of the non-Jewish thinkers of his day.

An exploration of Paul's understanding of sin will occupy us for the next two chapters. It will be crucial for the readers of these chapters to be willing to set aside—to forget for the moment—our own contemporary definitions and understanding of sin. Paul's definition is significantly different. So, whenever you see the word *sin* in these chapters, you will need to remind yourselves that it does not mean what you think it means. The letters are the same, but the meaning is very different.

This first chapter on sin will begin with a description of sin in terms of its emotional impact on us as humans. We will then turn to a definition of sin in terms of how it leads humans to misperceive their own lives as well as the lives of others. At the end of this chapter you should be able to give a brief definition of Paul's understanding of sin and to say something about the subjective impact of sin on human beings.

5

Sin

"I Do Not Do the Good I Want"

In our vocabulary, *sin* indicates some moral failing. We sin when we break a commandment or a law. So we speak of our sins, those occasions when we do something wrong or when we fail to do something right. In confession (in Christian churches), we list our sins. We make a list of all those thoughts or deeds that are in violation of the law. When we sin, the appropriate emotional response is guilt; the appropriate action is repentance. And because God is divine, God will forgive us. As indicated in the chapter on righteousness, this was the general understanding of the Judaism that nurtured Paul in the first century.[1] But it is also the general understanding of Christianity today.

Forgiveness is an important part of our lives. All of us can probably remember some time when a friend or a family member forgave us for something we did that put our relationship at risk. The experience of forgiveness helps us to understand that the relationships that constitute our life are ultimately more important than whether we are perfect. The confession of the people of Israel that YHWH is a forgiving God, a gracious and loving God, acknowledges that they know that their relationship with YHWH is crucial to life. When they violate this relationship by breaking their contract with God, YHWH will forgive them and welcome them back into the relationship if they repent. YHWH and Israel want to be in a relationship. Repentance and forgiveness are crucial elements in maintaining this relationship.

We often associate the words *repentance* and *forgiveness* with the message of Christianity: Through Jesus' death we are all forgiven for our sins; if we will repent and turn to God, then we can be in a relationship with God—for all eternity. So runs the message of Christianity. It may come as a surprise that this message of forgiveness sounds quite similar to the Judaism of Paul's day as well as the Judaism of our own.[2] Indeed, the structure is precisely the same: I sin (break a commandment), I experience guilt[3] because I stand under God's judgment, I repent, God forgives.

But there are some places in our society where this system has not helped us much. Indeed, we know that sometimes forgiveness is the inadequate, if not simply the wrong, response. The problem of spousal abuse has received much attention in our society in recent years. In these situations we can see clearly that the response of forgiveness worsens the deadliness of the situation, rather than offering any kind of salvation. A husband beats his wife. Afterward he repents, feeling sorrow for having lost his temper and hurt his wife.[4] She, taught well by her ostensibly Christian society, forgives her husband because she loves him. And all is well—until he loses his temper again. This cycle is repeated month after month, year after year. We can make all kinds of judgments against the man: He isn't truly sorry, he really is a louse, he doesn't deserve forgiveness. We can also make judgments against the woman: Why doesn't she leave him? Why doesn't she fight back? Eventually, if the woman is to survive, she probably has to leave him. But where does this leave the man? Forgiveness hasn't helped him. And he is likely to repeat the pattern with someone else.[5] Finally, we have come to realize that the man doesn't need forgiveness, he needs serious help. It is not just that he loses his temper. It is not just that he violates a commandment. The man who cannot keep himself from inflicting physical violence on his wife is sick—and no matter how often he repents, no matter how many times or how genuinely he is forgiven, the man, for some reason, slips back into the old destructive pattern.

What do we do when simple repentance of our sins doesn't change things but merely starts the same old cycle over again?[6] What do we do when, no matter how hard we try, we are still unable to live in right relationship? How can we ever live in right relationship if forgiveness doesn't work? Why does that clear process of justification given in Paul's tradition not lead to the justification it offers?

A DISEASE OF DESPERATION

Paul's understanding of sin describes such situations of impossibility. The beatings that an abusive husband inflicts upon his wife could be called sins. But Paul does not speak of sins in the plural. Nor does Paul talk about guilt, repentance, or forgiveness.[7] Rather, he speaks of the inability of the husband to change his behavior, and the corresponding inability of the wife to escape the abusive situation. Sin describes the whole situation of impossibility, not just the damaging or sinful acts that are symptoms of a deeper problem.

Listen to Paul describe the frustration in the experience of being a sinner:

> I do not understand my own actions. For I do not do what I want, but I do the very thing I hate. . . . For I do not do the good I want, but the evil I do not want is what I do. (Rom 7:15, 19)

The problem is not just that we do things that are wrong. Indeed, we do do things that are wrong. We break the law, and thus strain (or destroy) the relationship with God. As a Jew, Paul believed that all humans have this problem. All humans are sinners.[8] But as Paul understands it, the problem is not that people are sinners because they do wrong things. Rather, people do wrong things because they are sinners.

The situation that Paul describes is similar to that of alcoholism or drug addiction.

There may come a time when an alcoholic begins to recognize that her life is falling apart. She may sincerely want, at some level, to stop (or at least limit) drinking. She tells herself, "I do not want to get drunk tonight." But the very thing that she does not want to do is exactly what she does. Why is she unable to keep herself from drinking? Why do we "do the very thing we hate"? Paul gives this answer:

> Now if I do what I do not want, it is no longer I that do it, but sin which dwells within me. (Rom 7:20)

Why does the woman drink? We could say that it is not just that she has a problem with alcohol but, rather, that she has the disease of alcoholism. Paul's understanding of sin is similar to the assertion that alcoholism is a disease. The drinking (a sin) is a symptom of a disease (sin). There are those who fear that labeling alcoholism a disease will simply give the alcoholic one more excuse to continue drinking. Paul's own explanation why he does what he doesn't want to do seems also to be a convenient excuse: "The Devil made me do it!"

But there is something much more powerful at work here than simply giving explanations for destructive behavior that can absolve us of all responsibility. Many people in our society spend considerable money and time in therapy in order to understand why they have a particular problem in their lives. But understanding a problem is not enough. An alcoholic may understand that she is an alcoholic because of a physiological susceptibility to alcohol or because of a psychological formation. But she also must recognize that every time she takes a drink, she complies with the disease; she, in effect, says yes to the disease. And every time an alcoholic says yes, it is her fault. The same is true of sin. I may do the wrong things because of sin, but every time I comply with sin, I sin.

We may initially feel guilt in such situations, for we are aware that we are doing something wrong. We may try to stop drinking, to stop sinning, by the sheer strength of will. But if we try very many times, and fail every time, we begin to think that maybe something deeper is wrong with us. We may have the feeling that some alien force has taken us over and keeps us from doing what we want to do. Then our feelings may be more accurately described as despair, as utter helplessness. Such, at least, is Paul's description of life lived under the power of sin.

> Wretched man that I am! Who will deliver me from this body of death? (Rom 7:24)

The recognition that we are under the power of sin results in feelings of impotence. As one scholar has stated it, sin is "the inability to achieve that which it is desirable to achieve."[9] The alcoholic is unable

5:1 Struggling with Inability and Helplessness

1. What are some examples of things that you have really wanted to accomplish and have worked hard at but have nevertheless failed to achieve? Describe the way this failure made you feel.
2. Has there been a time when you have honestly tried to do the right thing in order to make a relationship with another person work out, but the more you tried, the worse the relationship got? Describe the experience.

to achieve the sobriety that she desires. The abusive husband is unable to achieve a life where he doesn't lose control. Oddly, however, it is not only the alcoholic or the abusive husband who is unable to achieve the desired life. The family of the alcoholic is equally unable to achieve a life without the damage of alcoholism. The abused spouse is unable to achieve a life of love and safety with her husband. The power of sin, like the power of righteousness, is corporate and relational. What looks to us like the sin of an individual, addiction, abuse, affects and is affected by the actions and the lives of other people.

In Paul's system of thought, we are unable to achieve that which is most desirable—righteousness. For Paul as a Jew, life consisted of being in a covenant relation with YHWH. Thus, sin, for Paul, is most evident in the inability to be in right relationship with God. Sin so determines human existence[10] that even when we want to be in right relation, even when we try to be in right relation, we are unable to attain a good relationship.

We experience this frustration occasionally in our relationships with other people. Have you ever had an argument or fight with a friend or a family member and found that the harder you tried to make things right again, the worse things got? Sin is not just a description of the brokenness that we sometimes experience in relationships. It is more. It describes that frustrating inability to achieve a reconciliation, even when that is what we most want.

Such is the case, according to Paul, in our relationship with God. The harder we try, the more estranged we become. It is as though there is an impenetrable barrier between us. You might think of it as something like a force field that repels in both directions in a science fiction movie.

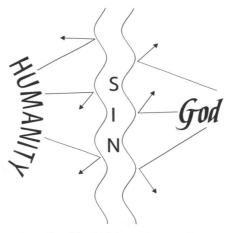

Illustration 8
Sin as a Force Field

Sin acts like a "force field" that repels even our best efforts to be in right relation with God. Note that it is not just that we cannot get through to God; God also is "frustrated" in efforts to get through to us.

How does such an impossible situation come about? How do we come to be so hopelessly alienated from what we most desire? As Paul says, "I do not understand my own actions" (Rom 7:15). What is the reason for our helplessness and despair?

MISPERCEIVING REALITY

We already know Paul's answer to the question, Why do we feel helpless and desperate? Sin is the name of our disease. But Paul uses other language to describe this disease. He writes, for instance, about the destructiveness of living "according to the flesh":

> For those who live according to the flesh set their minds on the things of the flesh . . . [and] to set the mind on the flesh is death. . . . For this reason the mind that is set on the flesh is hostile to God; it does not submit to God's law—indeed it cannot; and those who are in the flesh cannot please God. (Rom 8:5–8)

This is the culprit that sets us against God and results in our desperate sense of helplessness: We live according to the flesh; we set our minds on the things of the flesh. What, then, does Paul mean when he speaks about living "according to the flesh"?

The word *flesh* in Paul is often used in a technical sense. The Greek word *sarx*, which means "flesh," can mean simply the physical material that makes up our bodies, but Paul frequently uses the term in a specific, theological sense.[11] He contrasts living "according to the flesh" with living "according to the Spirit" (Rom 8:5–8). Now, Paul does not mean to imply that physical reality is somehow evil and spiritual reality is good. This is the way Paul has often been interpreted, and many Christians have expressed such a belief. But this understanding does not do justice to Paul's view of things.

In Paul's vocabulary, when he speaks of living according to the flesh versus living according to the Spirit, he is describing two opposing ways of understanding human life. To live according to the flesh means to perceive life from a limited human standpoint. To live according to the Spirit means to perceive life from the standpoint of God, the One who created life. Our helplessness derives from our misperception of human life and reality.

Misperceiving Our Humanity

Paul never denigrates flesh or humanity. Rather, he makes a judgment against living according to the flesh. It is, in Paul's view, not bad to be human. It is simply human to be human. It is good to have human drives, human ideas, and human aspirations. Paul never rejects our humanity. The problem he describes as living according to the flesh is, rather, that we misperceive our own humanity. We look to other humans ("flesh") to define our humanity rather than trusting our Creator's ("Spirit") definition of our humanity.

You might recall the ancient story of Adam and Eve in the garden of Eden. God had created humans to live in perfect harmony with God and all of creation. But Eve and Adam disobeyed God and were expelled from the garden. What was it that tempted them to disobey and to put at jeopardy all the glories of their life in Eden? The answer is surprising in some ways. The serpent had suggested to them that if they ate the fruit of the tree of the knowledge of good and evil, they would "be like God" (Gen 3:5). They disobeyed because they weren't content to be humans! God valued their humanity. There is no suggestion in the story that God dis-

---

5:2 The Ancient Tragedy (Genesis 3)

Now the serpent was more subtle than any other wild creature that the LORD God had made. He said to the woman, "Did God say, 'You shall not eat of any tree of the garden'?" And the woman said to the serpent, "We may eat of the fruit of the trees of the garden; but God said, 'You shall not eat of the fruit of the tree which is in the midst of the garden, neither shall you touch it, lest you die.' " But the serpent said to the woman, "You will not die. For God knows that when you eat of it your eyes will be opened, and you will be like God, knowing good and evil." So when the woman saw that the tree was good for food, and that it was a delight to the eyes, and that the tree was to be desired to make one wise, she took of its fruit and ate; and she also gave some to her husband, and he ate. Then the eyes of both were opened, and they knew that they were naked; and they sewed fig leaves together and made themselves aprons.

liked their humanity or thought it was insufficient or that God wanted them to be something other than human. No, it was Adam and Eve's own idea (albeit suggested by the serpent) that somehow it would be better for them to be something other than human.

This, it seems to me, strikes right at the heart of something that happens to each of us. Do you remember how, when you were in preschool, you would look longingly at your older brothers and sisters who got to bring homework home from school? It made them look so grown up! Or perhaps you can recall how jealous you were when your siblings or older friends were able to drive or have a job but because of your age you were not allowed to do these grown-up things. I remember well the frequent and well-aimed attack that we junior-high girls made against someone we disliked: "She's so immature!" What a revelation when it finally dawned on me that, to some degree, it was not only reasonable but appropriate that a sixth-grader should be immature in comparison with a seventeen-year-old! Why should a sixth-grader act like a junior in high school? It seems difficult for us to be willing to be where we are. Instead we envy those who seem to be stronger and better than we are. We miss out on portions of our own lives be-cause we are so eager to get to the next stage. Those ahead of us in life seem like gods, and we would far rather be like them than be who we already are.

Unfortunately, we don't simply outgrow this envy. Perhaps we eventually stop envying those who are older than us. But we still envy other people. We envy their jobs, their marriages, their children, their wealth, their talents, their houses. How frequently we imagine that "if only I had what that person has," life would be better, I would be happier. We do not trust our own lives. We find it impossible to believe that our lives are a gift from a good Creator. Something is always lacking. And who better to blame than the Creator? Unable to accept the sufficiency of our own place in life, we become hostile to the One who seems to withhold all those things that would make life better. We live "according to the flesh," that is, according to our own longing to be something other than we are, instead of accepting the goodness of what is given to us. The Creator intends for life to be good. But we, focusing our eyes on those who appear to be stronger, richer, and more gifted than we are, perceive the Creator as stingy and restraining. This is the true origin of our misperception of ourselves and of each other, according to Paul. It is not just that we misperceive who we are.

5:3 Misperceiving Ourselves

1. Describe a time when you were envious of someone older than you. Imagine that you are talking to someone who is just now at the age that you were then and has expressed to you an envy similar to the one you felt when you were younger. What would you say to this person?
2. Make two lists: one of all the things or abilities that you really wish you had, another of all the things and abilities that you already have. Which list was easier for you to make?
3. Ask a friend if he or she would be willing to write an honest description of you. Then respond to that description. Is this how you see yourself? What differences do you see between the ways others perceive you and the way you perceive yourself?

This misperception is simply the result of a greater misperception: We misperceive the One who has created us.

Misperceiving God the Creator

In Romans 1, Paul gives a long description of the character of sinful humanity, which elicits the wrath of God:

> For the wrath of God is revealed from heaven against all ungodliness and wickedness of those who by their wickedness suppress the truth. For what can be known about God is plain to them, because God has shown it to them. Ever since the creation of the world God's invisible nature, namely, God's eternal power and deity, has been clearly perceived in the things that have been made. So they are without excuse; for although they knew God they did not honor him as God or give thanks to God, but they became futile in their thinking and their senseless minds were darkened. Claiming to be wise, they become fools, and exchanged the glory of the immortal God for images resembling mere mortal human beings or birds or animals or reptiles.

> Therefore God gave them up in the lusts of their hearts to impurity, . . . because they exchanged the truth about God for a lie and worshiped and served the creature rather than the creator, who is blessed forever! Amen. (Rom 1:18–25)

Here Paul indicates that humans are sinful because they refuse to acknowledge God as God. We have exchanged the truth for a lie. We sin because we are confused about who we are, about the nature of life, and about the character of God. At its deepest, the problem that Paul calls sin derives from our misperception of God. We know that God is good, that God is loving and gracious. But no matter how much we may hear or want to believe that God has intended good for us, for some reason we cannot help but respond to God as some kind of ogre, as someone who judges us and punishes us because we are unable to live up to God's standards, standards that frequently appear to be both unfair and impossible to attain.

We know this dynamic well as teenagers. We may know, somewhere in our hearts, that our parents love us. But we cannot help but perceive that they are trying to control us with all their rules and restrictions. Our parents offer what they may intend as a helpful suggestion, but we respond as though it is just one more intrusion of them into our lives. We respond to their efforts to help as though they don't trust us to be able to do things ourselves. Our parents do not look like gracious, loving, merciful characters; rather, they appear to be "ruining my life!" We joke about how much our parents "learned" in six short years—from the time we were sixteen until we became twenty-two. We joke about it, because we know that it was not primarily the parent who changed but we who changed, and thus our perception of the parent changed. We have misperceived the parent. The character of the parent has not changed. The parent intended good all along. The problem was not that the parent suddenly changed into an evil being when we were sixteen. The problem was that we perceived the parent as someone who was against us.[12]

The same thing happens to us concerning God. God's character has not changed since God first made a covenant with Israel. God has always been righteous. God has always been in love with this people Israel. God has always been a merciful and forgiving God. But according to Paul, we have come to perceive God as someone who is against us. We have misperceived God so severely that God appears to be someone who is seeking to destroy us. Somehow we lose sight of the joy of that vision of shalom. We forget that we have signed on to a partnership

5:4 Misperceiving Our Parents

1. Describe a time when someone—either your parents or a friend or other family member—tried to offer you a helpful suggestion but you only felt as though they were interfering. Why did you perceive them as interfering? What kept you from considering their suggestion rationally?
2. For some of us, there seem to be particularly sensitive areas where it is almost impossible for someone close to us to give us advice—even if the advice is good and helpful advice. What are some of your trigger points? And who can most easily trigger them?

with this righteous God. Not experiencing either the righteousness (right relationship) or the shalom that God promises, we question God's own righteousness, we doubt God's own ability to bring real shalom into our world and into our lives. Just as children grow up to forget the simple joy of being held in their mother's arms, so we forget the truth of God's empowering love. The parent/God becomes foreign to us. And so, alienated from the joy that we once knew and yet have now forgotten and perhaps out-

grown, we not only feel helpless; we become hostile[13] to this God/parent who appears to withhold the longed-for love, security, and shalom.

What happens to us that makes us forget those early moments of love? Why, when someone loves us, do we reject this love and insist instead that they are against us? What is it that interferes, so to speak, in our ability to love and trust God? The surprising answer to these questions will be addressed in the next chapter.

READING CHECK:

☑   Why does forgiveness not always work? Why is misperception a problem that forgiveness cannot easily address?

☑   How is sin like a disease?

☑   How is sin related to a feeling of helplessness? Why does sin lead to feelings of despair? To feelings of hostility?

☑   What does it mean to live "according to the flesh"?

☑   What led to Eve and Adam's disobedience in the garden of Eden?

*I*n this chapter you will discover that the origin of our misperception of God and of our humanity is a surprising one. Paul links the power of sin directly to our human understanding of the law. There are only two logical responses to a law once it has been enacted: Either you obey or you disobey. But Paul says that neither obedience nor disobedience will ensure the righteousness that we desire. This chapter describes the disobedient response to the law as arising out of autonomy, and the obedient response as arising out of heteronomy. What do these two words mean—*autonomy* and *heteronomy?* At the end of this chapter you should be able to define these two words and describe how autonomy and heteronomy interact to form what Paul calls "the curse of the law."

6

Slavery and Death

"The Power of Sin Is the Law"

In the last chapter we learned that it is impossible to be in right relationship with someone when we misperceive who we are and who they are. The illustration about the abusive marriage can serve as an example. The abused wife can forgive her husband, but as long as he misperceives her as someone who interferes with his life, then he will never be able to be in right relationship with her. The man's perception of himself and of his wife will need to be changed in order for there to be change. Her forgiveness by itself does not change his misperception. Similarly, the woman's perception of both herself and her husband is perverted: Perhaps she perceives herself as somehow worthy of the abuse, and her husband as someone who really does love her.

What is it that leads us to misperceive ourselves and God so terribly? Paul says that we all misperceive: We are all sinners (Rom 3:23). What is it about human exis-

tence that causes us to do such damage to ourselves and others? The answer he gives is a surprising one.

In Romans 7 Paul makes it clear that it is the law that arouses sin. Read the following quotation carefully, for we will refer to it several times in the section that follows.

> While we were living in the flesh, our sinful passions, aroused by the law, were at work in our members to bear fruit for death. . . .
>
> What, then, shall we say? That the law is sin? Absolutely not! Yet, if it had not been for the law, I should not have known sin. I should not have known what it is to covet if the law had not said, "You shall not covet." But sin, seizing opportunity in the commandment, wrought in me all kinds of covetousness. Apart from the law sin lies dead. I was once alive apart from the law, but when the commandment came, sin revived and I died; the very commandment which promised life proved to be death to me. For sin, seizing

opportunity in the commandment, deceived me and by it killed me. So the law is holy, and the commandment is holy and just and good. (Rom 7:5, 7–12)

The last statement of this quote should remind you of what you read in the chapter on law. The law brings joy and life. Obedience to the law, though it may be a burden at times, is always worth the effort because it is through obedience to this gracious covenant with YHWH that we know shalom. Thus, Paul's statement that the law is "holy and just and good" is not at all a surprising statement.

What is surprising, indeed, almost bizarre, is that this statement comes at the conclusion to a paragraph on how the law arouses sin. If it is the law that arouses sin, then how can the law be "holy and just and good"? If the law that "promised life" proves, instead, "to be death to me," then how can Paul believe that the law is holy? Wouldn't we want to be rid of something that so deceived us by promising life when it in fact proves to be death? Since we know sin only because of the presence of the law, wouldn't it be best simply to throw the law out? Yet Paul adamantly refuses to accept this solution to the problem he poses. He appears to be contradictory here, unwilling to draw the obvious conclusion to his own argument. But let us not write Paul off so easily. For his dual insistence that (a) the law arouses sin and (b) the law is holy is crucial to his whole system of thought. Indeed, one of Paul's most creative insights arises out of his insistence that both of these statements are true. What does Paul understand to be the relationship between sin and the law?

It might help to return to the analogy of the law as a "syllabus" that God has given to Israel. In an academic course, the syllabus frequently lays out specific requirements of the students. Similarly, a job description details the specific expectations of you when you are hired. Such requirements stipulate what you, as student or employee, must do in order to perform in a satisfactory manner. In my own experience as teacher, although I sometimes enjoy challenging my students to create their own requirements, I certainly see advantages for the students in giving them a syllabus with stated requirements. Such requirements free the students from having to spend time figuring out what would be most helpful for them in learning the material for the course. The students generally have much less anxiety about what is necessary in the course when I have already spelled it out for them. The syllabus provides a bit more security for them if they are uncertain about how best to study the material. The problem with a syllabus, however, is that once you enroll in the course, you only have two choices with regard to the syllabus. If a final paper is assigned, you either write it or refuse to write it. You don't really have a choice about whether you have to write the paper. You may choose not to write the paper; but this choice will surely result in a failing grade (and wasted time and money for the course). But if the requirements are left up to you, whether you write a final paper is not in itself important.

The same is true of the law. Once the law is given, there are only two possible responses: Either we obey it or disobey it. Once the law is present, it has to be dealt with. The problem, according to Paul, is that neither of the two possible responses to the law works to bring about righteousness. Let's look more closely at these two responses to the law and see if we can understand how each response fails to accomplish the goal of righteousness.

REBELLION: AUTONOMY LEADS TO DEATH

This response to the law is the most obviously sinful response. From our earliest days as a toddler, we learn that defying Mother's no! is likely to get us into trouble. The consequences for rebellion against law are frequently obvious. If I speed on the highway (and get caught), the consequence is that my bank account will have $100 less in it. If you refuse to write the final paper required for a course, you will flunk the course. Similarly, Israel understood that if it refused to obey the commandments of the law, there would be negative consequences. See, for example, the extensive list of curses found in Deuteronomy 28:

> If you will not obey the LORD your God by diligently observing all his commandments and decrees, which I am commanding you today, then all these curses shall come upon you and overtake you: . . .
>
> The LORD will send upon you disaster, panic, and frustration in everything you attempt to do, until you are destroyed and perish quickly, on account of the evil of your deeds, because you have forsaken me. (Deut 28:15, 20)

Rebellion against the law clearly has serious consequences! The question that we need to explore is, Why? Are the "curses" that result from disobeying the law arbitrary? Are they simply punishments inflicted by some authority for your failure to play by the rules? Or is there some inner connection between the consequences and the failure to observe the law?

The Impulse to Disobey: Identity through Separation

We may feel at times as though the consequences of our rebellion are arbitrarily given by those in authority. In some cases, this is no doubt true. But in principle, when you flunk a course for which you refused to write the final paper, it is not because the professor doesn't like you or because the teacher wants to punish you. If you are fired for failing to perform the required tasks for your job, you are simply reaping the results of your own failure to uphold your part of the covenant. The failing grade or loss of job simply reflects the reality: You have not been faithful to your commitment.

If the consequences of disobedience are so obvious, and in some cases so dire, why do we disobey? Do we consciously choose to disobey? Paul would suggest that our disobedience is not due to a conscious choice to disobey (look back at Rom 7:15). And yet we do disobey.

The toddler may learn early on that defying Mother's no! can result in trouble for him. But the toddler also learns quickly that he, too, can say, no! It seems to be a universal experience that toddlers think it is their duty to test every no! that the parent gives. Imagine that a youngster is crawling around a room. As the phone rings in the next room

---

6:1 Compelled to Disobey

1. Think about how the very presence of the law can compel us to disobey. List several examples of how you have rebelled against the rules. (These can be simple examples—no need to convict yourself of a felony here.)
2. For each instance you listed above, which of these things did you do because you truly wanted to do them, and which did you probably do simply because someone told you not to? Be honest! Are there any you perhaps would not even have thought about doing if you had not been told not to do them?
3. Place a check mark by those that were acts of compulsive rebellion against the law.

and you get up to answer it, you notice that the child is headed straight for an electrical outlet. You quickly rush to the child, point to the outlet, and forcefully say, "No-no. Don't touch. Hurt baby." Then you rush out of the room to answer the ringing telephone. What do you suppose will be the first thing that child will do when you leave the room? Straight for the outlet!

This impulse is not limited to the toddler years. We experience it, in greater or lesser degrees, throughout our lives. Paul acknowledges this when he says, "I should not have known what it is to covet if the law had not said, 'You shall not covet.' But sin, finding opportunity in the commandment, wrought in me all kinds of covetousness" (Rom 7:7–8). The very fact that the law says, "Don't covet," makes me want to covet. We may pass by a bench in a park a hundred times without feeling any need to touch it. But let someone put a sign on that bench that says, "Wet Paint," and we are suddenly fiercely tempted to touch the bench. This is not a rational process. It is as though something compels us to disobey. The simple presence of the law sometimes goads us to disobedience.

In the cases of both the toddler and the "Wet Paint" sign, it seems that we need somehow to see for ourselves. We don't want simply to accept someone else's experience or knowledge. We need to experience the world—both the good and the bad—for ourselves. Otherwise, how will we truly know what the truth is? This experience of testing the world is frequently intensified in adolescence and young adulthood. It is not uncommon for people to explain so-called teenage rebellion as a necessary effort on the part of adolescents to find their own identity. As adolescents we don't want simply to accept the identity that our parents have given to us. We often try out several different identities. And sometimes this means trying out identities that are very different from, or even opposed to, the identity that mommy and daddy have given to us. We declare, "You don't understand me! You don't know who I am! I am not who you think I am!"

In our society we often define maturity as autonomy.[1] How will I know that my children have grown up? When they can stand on their own two feet. The problem is, however, that in order for my children to be autonomous, they must develop their own identities, identities that are separate from my identity. They must, to some degree, rebel against me. Psychologists sometimes

6:2 St. Augustine and the Pear Tree Theft

In his Confessions St. Augustine tells a story about how, as a youth, he reveled in stealing simply because of the joy of rebellion.

I was willing to steal, and steal I did, although I was not compelled by any lack. . . . For of what I stole I already had plenty, and much better at that, and I had no wish to enjoy the things I coveted by stealing, but only to enjoy the theft itself and the sin. There was a pear-tree near our vineyard, loaded with fruit that was attractive neither to look at nor to taste. Late one night a band of ruffians, myself included, went off to shake down the fruit and carry it away, for we had continued our games out of doors until well after dark, as was our pernicious habit. We took away an enormous quantity of pears, not to eat them ourselves, but simply to throw them to the pigs. Perhaps we ate some of them, but our real pleasure consisted in doing something that was forbidden. (Augustine, Confessions 4.9, Ryan)[2]

refer to this process of separation as individuation. All of us need somehow to come to see ourselves as individuals who are separate from our parents. This is a natural process, but it is not a simple one. Indeed, as many will attest, it is a deeply complicated process, one that can and often does cause both parents and children much pain and some anger.

The Failure of Autonomy

Paul would say that this pain and anger occur because there is a fundamental problem with the process of individuation through rebellion. He would agree that it is a natural process. But this process necessarily results in a limitation of our freedom (slavery) as well as in the pain of alienation (death). This pain is not punishment for the rebellion; it is the natural consequence of striving to establish one's own individual identity apart from that which gives us life.

Remember the example in chapter 3 about the law of becoming a professional dancer? Imagine that at a very young age you had been taken to dance lessons and your parents noticed that you not only were good at dancing but seemed to come alive when you danced. So your parents, desiring to cultivate your joy, made a commitment to do whatever they could to encourage you in a life of dance. But as you grew older, even though you continued to excel in dance, you began to resent your parents' insistence that you practice, and you began to resist your dance instructor's training.[3] You began to look longingly at the free time that your nondancing friends had, and you wished you could just rebel against your parents and your instructor and discover for yourself what you really wanted in life. So you quit your dance lessons; indeed, you quit dancing altogether. You no longer submit to the "law of dance" but search instead for "your own law" (autonomy).

What is the result of your newfound "freedom"? Well, you may be free of the demands of being a dancer. But you have lost the freedom of what had once been your greatest joy. If, for some reason, you wished you could suddenly change your mind and begin dancing again, then you would have to swallow your pride and admit that your parents and your instructor had been right all along. And to do that would destroy the very autonomy that you had been seeking to establish. So you are now free to do anything . . . but dance. Your rebellion against your parents (and their discipline) has ironically enslaved you to a life without dance. You are alienated from the one thing that had brought you joy. At the age of thirty you look back and see that you have lost your prime dancing years, wasting your time on other much less enjoyable things, struggling to find your own way when the way had been there all along. You have lost, now, the freedom to dance. The dancing you is dead.

As you will recall from part 1, Israel affirmed that life is found precisely in covenantal relation with YHWH. Disobeying the law of this covenant, even if it is for the good purpose of knowing the truth for oneself, results in death because human wholeness and truth can be known only in relation to others, to God, and to our own deepest desires. In sin as autonomy the individual buys his or her identity at the cost of damaging or even destroying the relationship. But life without relationship to the giver of life is death. So, the consequence of sin as autonomy is death, not as some arbitrary punishment for rebelling against a dictatorial authority but as the inevitable result of rebelling against God's shalom. Thus, sin leads to death.[4] It is unavoidable.

Paul's understanding of death needs fuller explanation. But before we can understand the depth of the agony of death, we need first to take a look at the other possible response to the law.

ADHERENCE: HETERONOMY ALSO LEADS TO DEATH!

If rebellion against the law leads to death, then surely the way to avoid death is to adhere to the law. This is, indeed, what many of us have been taught. But Paul adamantly rejects this conclusion. Paul declares that adhering to the law does not bring life but, rather, results in death, just as surely as rebelling against the law results in death. As Robin Scroggs says, the pious person "is not a sinner when he fails to fulfill the law; somehow he is a sinner precisely when he does fulfill the law."[5] This is one of Paul's most creative insights.[6] It is surely one that sets him apart from the general Jewish view of his day.

Why is Paul so insistent that obedience to the law does not lead to life? What is it that leads him to deny the relationship between law and righteousness, a relationship that his tradition has so strongly affirmed? If you followed the argument above about why autonomy leads to death, you already have some clues on how Paul's logic necessarily led him to this insight. Let's take a closer look at the dynamics inherent in obeying the law.

The Impulse to Obey: Identity through Connection

While we may think it is the natural and inevitable experience of being human to rebel against authority, there are, in fact, indications that this is not the overwhelming experience of life for many people. Parents may dread the years of the terrible twos or of teenage rebellion. But sometimes these years turn out to be not so bad after all. Parents may say of one of their children, "She has never given us a moment's trouble." Believe it or not, there are some who go through the teenage years without ever really rebelling against their parents. The journey from childhood to adulthood seems to be a fairly smooth one. How can this be so?

It is perhaps impossible to explain why some children seem compelled to rebel and others seem perfectly happy to obey. But it would be difficult to deny that such differences exist. We have seen that the primary impetus of rebellion lies in the desire to establish an independent identity. The impetus of obedience surely expresses a desire to please. But there is another, deeper motivation in persistent obedience: Through following the commandment, we can be assured of remaining secure and safe in the relationship. There is nothing wrong with wanting to please those who have given us life (just as there is nothing wrong with wanting to establish an identity). There is nothing wrong with the desire to be safe. The obedient one has an inherent ability to trust. She accepts the identity and the reality given to her by her parents. She feels no need to question it. Obeying her parents brings results she can, indeed, trust. She sees the pride in their eyes; she hears the pleasure in their voices. And every time she does, her impulse to obey, to please her parents deepens and intensifies her sense of security.

The obedient child does have an identity. It is not one that she has carved out for herself; it is, rather, one that comes through being in a secure relationship with her parents. She is who they want her to be—and everyone is pleased. There are people who are not autonomous and do not desire to be autonomous. Indeed, autonomy (separation) looks like death to them. In the United States, the rush to join sororities and fraternities on many college campuses gives some evidence that we will do almost anything in order to be a part of a group—and avoid the

---

6:3 Desperately Seeking Security

All of us at some time or other have been afraid to be ourselves with one of our friends for fear that our friend would reject us if he or she knew who we really were. What are some things you have done in order to gain the approval of your friends or parents?

---

dreaded curse of being alone. Autonomy sometimes sounds better than it feels. We choose to efface our own individuality in order to be accepted by others. In such situations our goal would be better described by *heteronomy*[7] than *autonomy*. Others determine our lives, not self. We live according to the expectations of someone else. We adhere to the law of another, accepting the secure identity that such a law provides for us. Indeed, a major element in this pattern is a desire for security.

The dynamic of heteronomy is sometimes difficult to see. On the one hand, since the drive for autonomy is the norm for our society,[8] it is sometimes embarrassing for us to admit, even to ourselves, that we are afraid to stand on our own. On the other hand, heteronomy often looks to us like what God (and everyone else) wants of us: Obey! We have been taught well. And it is difficult for us to look at those teachings (especially the religious teachings) in a more critical light. But if we are ever to understand Paul, we have to make the effort to see why he says that heteronomy fails to produce either healthy human life or the righteousness that we seek.

The Failure of Heteronomy

Paul insists that there is no salvation in keeping the law. He makes this especially clear in his letter to the churches of Galatia:

Now it is evident that no one is justified before God by the law. (Gal 3:11b)

If a law had been given which could make alive, then righteousness would indeed be by the law. (Gal 3:21b)

Paul questions the law because it does not accomplish what it promised. As he tells the Romans, although the people of Israel had the law and kept the law, they nevertheless "failed to obtain what they sought" (Rom 11:7). The law, which promised life, instead brought death.

Why does the law fail to fulfill the promise of righteousness? The answer for Paul is, of course, sin. But what dynamics keep us from experiencing the life that obedience to the law is supposed to bring? Why does heteronomy fail?

In Rom 7:7–12, where Paul declares that "the very commandment which promised life proved to be death to me," he twice indicates that sin "seizes opportunity in the commandment." The failure of heteronomy lies precisely in this seizure of the commandment. The reasoning of heteronomy is as follows: "The commandment promises life and security for me; thus, if I grab hold of the commandment and hold on to it for dear life, I will have life and security. I will do what it says. I will obey it in every way. What could be more secure than always doing exactly what God tells me to?"[9]

This reasoning reminds me of an episode in the television series *Star Trek: The Next Generation*, where Data (a human-looking computer/robot) plays the violin in a concert for the crew of the *Enterprise*. Being a computer, he plays the violin meticulously. But he does not play the violin musically. He plays all the notes (and there are lots of them) perfectly. His timing is perfect. His technique is perfect. But it isn't music. Sometimes I see this same dynamic in teaching. I give the students instructions: "Do this. Don't do that." And my instructions are good, reliable instructions. But every now and then, I get a paper turned in where the student does exactly what I told him to, but it is not a good paper. Other students follow the same instructions and do write good papers. It is always very difficult to explain to the student what the problem is. I find myself saying, "Yes, I did tell you to do that. But you did it too much" or "you did it in the wrong way." What I want to say is, "Yes, I did tell you to do that. But you have got to use some of your own independent sense as to how and when to do it." But the student, so worried about making a good grade, is afraid to use his independent sense and instead thinks that following the rules will assure him a good grade. I also see this dynamic in the ways that students take notes on lectures. Many students are afraid that they will miss something, something that will be on the exam, and so they try to write down everything I say. But the students' fear means that they are so busy writing down the words that they are not able to pay attention to the ideas. They are not thinking with me. And thus their work on exams looks like so much regurgitation. They have missed the connections between the words.

We could say that my students sometimes seize the words but miss the point. Or that

Data seized the notes but failed to make music. The failure of heteronomy is that we seize the law but miss out on the righteousness.

The irony in this "seizure of the commandment" is that although we thought we were seizing the law, we soon discover that the law has instead seized us: We have become slaves of the law. And our enslavement prohibits our participation in what we most want. Data's slavish attention to the notes prevented him from playing music. The students become enslaved by my instructions and thus are hindered from writing good papers. What is needed is that Data and the students dare to put some of themselves into their playing and writing. They must even dare, for the sake of music, for the sake of a good paper, to go beyond the rules.

The same daring is needed for there to be a strong relationship between people. If we always go along with what the other person wants, then there is no real relationship. The joy of relationship lies precisely in the fact that two distinct persons are involved. There is you and there is me, and our relationship is fun and meaningful not only because we have some desires in common but also because we are different. If you always go along with me, then we have no relationship.

Paul's tradition provided him with ample illustration of the kind of daring that made for a strong relationship with YHWH. Abraham had dared to challenge God's decision to destroy Sodom and Gomorrah (see sidebar 6:6). Moses, too, dared to fight with God when God threatened to desert Israel (see

6:4 Seizing the Commandment

1. What are some examples where you (or others) followed the rules meticulously but failed to accomplish good results?
2. Can you think of some examples of how it is sometimes necessary to go beyond (and maybe even violate) some rules in order to achieve the desired ends?

6:5 An Allegory of Slavery and Freedom (Gal 4:22–26)

For it is written that Abraham had two sons, one by a slave woman and the other by a free woman. One, the child of the slave, was born according to the flesh; the other, the child of the free woman, was born through the promise. Now this is an allegory: these women are two covenants. One woman, in fact, is Hagar, from Mount Sinai, bearing children for slavery. Now Hagar is Mount Sinai in Arabia and corresponds to the present Jerusalem, for she is in slavery with her children. But the other woman corresponds to the Jerusalem above; she is free, and she is our mother.

Numbers 14). The book of Job records at length how the pious man Job argued his case vehemently against God. These heroes of the faith were singular persons with strong identities, able to be in a relationship with YHWH and yet challenge him when they disagreed.

The heteronomous impulse to submit to the other in order to nurture and maintain the relationship finally results not in a relationship but in an enslavement to the idea of a relationship. That is, an active relationship depends upon there being at least two persons. But if I do not have a secure sense of my own identity, I am not able to be a person in a relationship. I become enslaved (or addicted) to my need for your approval. I am afraid to disagree or to assert my own wishes. Fearing that any argument will destroy the "relationship," I squelch my own identity and become enslaved to what I think you want. Indeed, this enslavement becomes my identity. I can only be a "we," not an "I."

The problem is, our society teaches us that the only way to be a person, a person with a distinct identity as an individual self, is to rebel. And such rebellion is impossible for those of us who are addicted to approval. Independence would put our security at risk,

6:6 Abraham Challenges God (Gen 18:23–31)

Then Abraham drew near, and said, "Wilt thou indeed destroy the righteous with the wicked? Suppose there are fifty righteous within the city; wilt thou then destroy the place and not spare it for the fifty righteous who are in it? Far be it from thee to do such a thing, to slay the righteous with the wicked, so that the righteous fare as the wicked? Far be that from thee! Shall not the judge of all the earth do right?" And the LORD said, "If I find at Sodom fifty righteous in the city, I will spare the whole place for their sake." Abraham answered, "Behold, I have taken upon myself to speak to the Lord, I who am but dust and ashes. Suppose five of the fifty righteous are lacking? Wilt thou destroy the whole city for lack of five?" And he said, "I will not destroy it if I find forty-five there." Again he spoke to him, and said, "Suppose forty are found there." He answered, "For the sake of forty I will not do it." Then he said, "Oh let not the Lord be angry, and I will speak. Suppose thirty are found there." He answered, "I will not do it, if I find thirty there." He said, "Behold, I have taken upon myself to speak to the Lord. Suppose twenty are found there." He answered, "For the sake of twenty I will not destroy it." Then he said, "Oh let not the Lord be angry, and I will speak again but this once. Suppose ten are found there." He answered, "For the sake of ten I will not destroy it." (RSV)

especially when that security is dependent upon the approval of an authority—and even more so when that authority is God, who gives the law. "Wretched woman that I am. Who will deliver me from this dilemma?"

Constant observance of the law prevents us from developing our own identity. And although the purpose of the law is to enable our relationship with YHWH, we are unable to be in a genuine relationship with another, even with YHWH, if we have no identity as an individual. We have become so enslaved to the law that we have killed (or failed to develop) one of the key elements for a good relationship, our self. Thus, just as with autonomy, sin as heteronomy also results in our death.

"THE CURSE OF THE LAW"

It may seem as though we have completely abandoned the view of law articulated in chapter 3. In some ways we have. It is not as though this view of the law as a gracious gift is now wrong. Certainly Paul continues to think of the law as "holy and just and good." But our human vision of the law is faulty. Our misperception of what it means to be fully human affects the way we see the law. God gives the law as a gracious gift. But we, being human and living according to our own limited understanding of reality, see the law as something other than a gracious gift.

When we misperceive life as consisting of autonomy, we respond to the law as though it were trying to control us. And thus we rebel against it. The law may in fact be a gracious gift. But in our compulsion to establish our own identity, to find our own way, we cannot help but know that the law is just one more attempt to control us, to keep us from finding our own way. It seems arbitrary, out of touch with who we are, and so we fight against it. The law is intended as gift, but we perceive it as control.

When we misperceive life as consisting of heteronomy, we respond to the law as though it offers us security. Our assumption that obedience will result in righteousness functions perversely by tempting us to "seize the commandment" in order to be able to insure the relationship with God. But in our acquiescence we never experience the risk that healthy relationships entail. In our desperate attempt to find security, we yield blindly to the law; but then we never know what it means to engage the other (God) fully. The law is intended to bring us life and a full, vital, engaging relationship, but we perceive it as a way to be safe.

Our faulty human vision leads us to misperceive human life. This misperception is both pernicious (we don't know that we're wrong: "Our minds are darkened") and apparently unavoidable (all people we know misperceive themselves: "All have sinned"). It is no surprise, then, that Paul claimed that the power of this misperception was evidence of those mighty forces imagined in apocalyptic eschatology. The misperception is larger than just our individual misperception; it infects whole social institutions. We have, in our day, lost the language to talk about these unseen but real social (and psychological) forces that structure our misperception. But in Paul's day, he still had available such a language to describe the massiveness of our blindness. Our eyes have been blinded by the "principalities and powers" who have so obstructed our vision that even God's gracious gift of the law becomes something other than it is. It is no longer for us the way to righteousness but has become instead the very barrier to experiencing God's righteousness.

Paul, quoting Deut 27:26, declares to the Galatians,

> For all who rely on works of the law are under a curse; for it is written, "Cursed be every one who does not abide by all things

written in the book of the law, and do them."
(Gal 3:10)

Now, if we stop reading Paul at this point, we may well assume, given his citation of Deut 27:26, that the "curse of the law" lies in our inability to obey the law. After all, we reason, no one is perfect. But Paul argues that the curse of the law lies elsewhere. Indeed, Paul could describe himself by saying, "As to righteousness under the law, [I was] blameless!" (Phil 3:6). Paul's explanation of the curse follows his citation from Deuteronomy, when he says, "Now it is evident that no one is justified before God by the law" (Gal 3:11). It is not that we are unable to keep the law; rather, it is that, even in keeping the whole law, we fail somehow to achieve the righteousness with God that we desire. "Israel did not attain what it sought" (Rom 11:7). The very presence of the law (which is "holy and just and good"), because of the power of sin, bars us from the very righteousness that it offers.

Illustration 9
The Law as Barrier

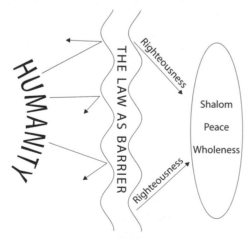

The law, which was meant to guide humanity to shalom, through the activity of God's righteousness, has instead become a barrier which prevents humanity from sharing God's righteous activity of bringing shalom.

If this is true about the law, then why do we not simply throw it over? Why not just walk away from the law? Why pay any attention to something that is impotent at best and destructive at worst? But such ability to ignore the law, once it is present, is not within our power. We might say that the curse of the law lies precisely in our inability to walk away from it. Whether we obey it or disobey it, we are still defined by it. We are unable not to care about the law, for it is through the law, both in disobedience and in obedience, that we are assured of response from the God who gives the law. When we obey the law, we can expect approval; when we rebel against the law, we can expect anger. Both of these actions and expectations reveal that, at our depths, we long for a relationship with the lawgiver. We hunger for response, for recognition.

The child who cleans her room wants, even expects, commendation from her parent. Cleaning the room is not satisfaction; only the parent's smile brings completion to the act. No less so for the child who willfully refuses the neatness the parent demands; his rebellion ensures the parent's continued response. In itself, the room, neat or not, is inconsequential (to the child, at least!). Its consequence is defined solely as it becomes a mediating battleground that assures a continued relation between parent and child. All that the child hungers for finds expression not in "Will I or will I not clean my room?" but, rather, in "How will I best ensure a response from my parent?"

Despite some recent court cases that would indicate otherwise, children cannot divorce their parents. That which has formed us is in us. We have no option, then, but to live in some relation to it. We cannot by choice make another our mother or our father. We cannot choose our parents. Nor can we unchoose them. Once created, we are always and forever creatures of these creators;

it cannot be otherwise. We may choose with our conscious minds to ignore our relation, but we cannot drain their blood from us. We may deafen our ears through distance and silence, but we cannot void the voices that we have memorized in minute detail. No amount of physical distance can separate us from those early touches, those long-ago voices. Our parents are forever embedded in us, and no divorce from them is possible. No surgical instrument can excise the creators from our marrow. We are because of them.

So it is with God. We cannot sidestep the law, because it bears witness to the imprint of God on our being. Death lies in our knowledge that we cannot divorce God: We cannot be independent. Yet we cannot seem to find a way to be ourselves in relation to this law-giving God. We hunger for God; we crave ourselves. This is the depth of sin revealed. For we simultaneously wish to be ourselves and long to be rightly related to the One who gives us life. We rebel in order to create ourselves; we obey in order to know relationship with the life giver. We are both autonomous and heteronomous at the same time, for every act of rebellious autonomy contains within it the seeds of defining ourselves in relation to another; and every act of compliant heteronomy is a cry for a recognition of self.

CONCLUSION

The pattern of sin-repentance-forgiveness is a system of justification that is built upon the law. But it is precisely the law that is the site of our sin—not because we always disobey the law but because we do not know how to perceive accurately either ourselves or the God who gives the law. God intends the law for good. But because of sin we perceive and experience the law as destructive.

Thus, as we are mired in our misperception, forgiveness appears to be (a) God's effort to control us (an autonomous response) or (b) a restoration to a false security with a God whom we misperceive (a heteronomous response). Neither rebellion against nor adherence to the law leads to righteousness, and since the purpose of the law was to lead us to righteousness, the reality of sin leaves us in a Catch-22 situation. Thus, not only are we helpless; we are also hostile to this law-giving God who has placed us in this impossible double bind.

The unavoidable result of sin is death. That is, misperception (of ourselves, of each other, of God) always results in an impossible situation. We become trapped in our own inability to perceive reality truly. This is death: the inescapable trap of misperception, living in a false reality, the inability to find our way home to true life. For we cannot force ourselves to perceive other than what we perceive. We cannot reason our way to new perception. Our only hope is that somehow "the true God" (the God beyond our misperception) will be revealed to us, apart from the law. And this revelation is precisely what Paul understood to take place in Christ.

READING CHECK:

☑ What is the problem with the law?

☑ Define and describe autonomy. Why does rebellion not lead to righteousness?

☑ Define and describe heteronomy. Why does adherence to the law not lead to righteousness?

☑ Relate the dynamics of autonomy and heteronomy to sarx ("flesh") and perception.

☑ What is the "curse of the law"?

part two

Summary and Review

SUMMARY

The Jewish ideas of shalom, righteousness, and law formed the foundation of Paul's thought. The interrelation of these three concepts also formed a strong basis for the Jewish community. This structure provided a coherent framework for the Jewish people, articulating their hopes and dreams, their passions, and a process for maintaining and renewing their community. But what of the rest of humanity? If the God of the Jewish people is the Creator of all, then how are the ideas of shalom, righteousness, and law related to those who stand outside the Jewish community?

During the period when Paul lived, these questions became sharply focused, perhaps especially so for the Jews who lived in the Diaspora. Paul himself had grown up in the Diaspora. We do not know whether Paul had a Greco-Roman education or whether he had engaged in conversation with any of the schools of Greco-Roman philosophy. But his thinking about sin and death shows that he was concerned about many of the same things that concerned these Gentile philosophers. Paul could have chosen to translate his Jewish understanding into the terms of the philosophers. Other Jews of this period attempted to do so. But Paul chose instead to reflect on these Gentile concerns within the language and terms of his Jewish heritage. This reflection in turn widened Paul's understanding of sin in relation to his own Jewish belief system.

Thus, Paul's understanding of sin takes on a peculiar character. Rather than defining sin only as the violation of the (Jewish) law, Paul expands the definition of sin to include Jews and Gentiles equally (see Romans 1–3). Paul's tradition had taught that sin is violation of the law and that repentance and God's forgiveness would return one to the covenant. For someone standing within the

Jewish community, someone who has accepted the full responsibility of obedience to Torah, this understanding of sin-repentance-forgiveness is perhaps sufficient. But Paul's thought assumes two prior questions: (1) What about those who have not bound themselves to the Jewish community and its law? One cannot repent (= return) to a community that one has never joined. And (2) why do even the Jews who "love the law" fail to realize righteousness? Even repentance does not seem to solve the problem of repetitious sin. In short, Paul asks, what is the underlying relation between law and sin?

As a result of Paul's encounter with Christ (see part 3), Paul began to rethink his own understanding of human life. He, like the philosophers, was convinced that human misery, whether in the Jewish experience or in the Gentile experience, was the result of human misperception. But unlike the philosophers', Paul's reflections on human misery were informed by his own commitment to the God of Israel and God's desire to bring shalom to all peoples. The goal was not human contentment but, rather, shalom for all God's creation.

It was of utmost importance, then, that Paul articulate the relation between this human misery and God's righteousness, the relation between human failure and God's law. According to Paul, Jews and Gentiles alike misunderstood the nature of God, and this resulted in their living impotent and pain-filled lives. This human misperception of God led humans to misunderstand God's good gift of law. In the confused desires to please self and to please God, humans had mistaken the function of the law, and the law itself became the barrier to experiencing God's righteousness. The law separated Jews and Gentiles; it enticed one to seek security in one's own obedience rather than in God; it seduced one into rebellion against the Creator.

Thus, although Paul's reflections on human misery address concerns that were shared by Greco-Roman philosophy, he articulated his own view in direct relation to his faith in the God of Israel. He used religious rather than philosophical terminology. He lived and worked in the Gentile world, but his life and work both emerged out of and were directed toward the hopes and fulfillment of YHWH's desire to bring shalom to the world through partnership with a people committed to the same dream of cosmic shalom.

REVIEW

A. Terms and Concepts

1. universal citizenship
2. Adam
3. original sin
4. perception/misperception
5. sin as disease
6. sin as misperception of God
7. sin as misperception of self
8. the curse of the law
9. *sarx*
10. flesh
11. autonomy
12. individuation
13. heteronomy
14. seizing the commandment
15. death
16. slavery

B. Making Connections

1. Reread the journal or essay you wrote at the conclusion of part 1. Then reflect on this question: What things might interfere with your dream and prevent you from fulfilling it? Devote a full paragraph to describing each potential interference. Is this interference avoidable? How? What things are under your control? What things

are not under your control? To what degree does your dream depend on other people? To what degree can other people interfere with and thwart your dream? Are there institutional or social barriers that might interfere? What might some of these be? If sin can be described as "the inability to achieve that which is desirable to achieve," how does this relate to your inability to achieve a dream? What feelings does this arouse in you?

2. Saint Augustine was an important interpreter of Paul's thought. He distinguished between sin and sins. The force of sin leads the individual to commit sinful acts. This distinction may help you relate Paul's notion of sin as a force to our more common understanding of sins as violations of a law. With this distinction between sin and sins in mind, reflect on the following set of questions in relation to the plot of a book, a movie, or even an episode of a sitcom.

(a) List some examples of *sins* in the story. What are some of the wrong acts that are committed? Why are they wrong? What are some mistakes that are made? Are they innocent mistakes or intentional misdeeds? What is the surface event that causes the conflict in the story? What is wrong that needs to be fixed?

(b) Now, see if you can identify *sin* that lies underneath the sins. Remember that, in Paul's view, sin is not so much something that we do wrong; it is a force that twists our good human desires (the desire to be a self, the desire to be safe) against us in destructive ways. Looking at the key sins in the story, what caused these misdeeds? In what ways might these sins be an expression of a basically good human desire gone awry?

3. Read the book *A Separate Peace* by John Knowles. Or watch the video of the movie based on this book. Write an essay in response to the following questions:

(a) What are some examples of sin as autonomy in this book?

(b) What are some examples of sin as heteronomy in this book?

(c) Is there any law expressed in this book? In what ways?

(d) What is the relation between sin and law in the book?

(e) Describe how sin and law affect the relation between Phineas and Gene.

You may want to consult Robert Jewett's book *Saint Paul at the Movies*, chapter 4.

Paul's Creative Contribution

A Redeemed World

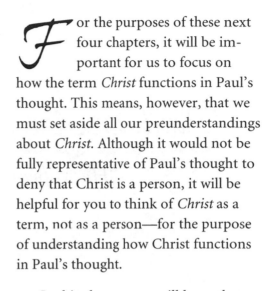

For the purposes of these next four chapters, it will be important for us to focus on how the term *Christ* functions in Paul's thought. This means, however, that we must set aside all our preunderstandings about *Christ*. Although it would not be fully representative of Paul's thought to deny that Christ is a person, it will be helpful for you to think of *Christ* as a term, not as a person—for the purpose of understanding how Christ functions in Paul's thought.

In this chapter you will learn that Paul's experience of Christ is central to his interpretation of human life. What are three ways that scholars have interpreted Paul's experience? What is Paul's own interpretation of his experience? By the end of this chapter you should be able to answer these questions and articulate a broad definition of the term *Christ*.

7

Paul, an Apostle of Christ Jesus

"He Appeared Also to Me"

Paul was a Jew who lived in the Greco-Roman world. The first two major parts of this study have outlined how Paul's heritage (Judaism) and social context (Greco-Roman) are reflected in his thought. None of us thinks in a vacuum. And certainly Paul's Judaism within a Greco-Roman context determined much about the contours of Paul's thought. But what if we were to ask Paul himself, "What, Paul, is the central and determining element in your thought?" Paul would probably not begin by delineating his heritage or his context. No, in Paul's own understanding, it was his experience of Christ that constituted the focus and the impetus of his intellectual work.

Although the purpose of this volume is not to summarize Paul's life but, rather, to portray his thought, it is nevertheless important to emphasize that Paul's thought was intimately related to his experience of Christ, an experience that transformed his life. Paul was a Jewish man who lived among, and ministered primarily to, Gentiles. The importance of this Jewish-Gentile mixture can be seen in the quotation from Galatians below. Paul acknowledges that he was "advanced in Judaism." But the revelation of Christ persuaded Paul that God had called him to "proclaim him among the Gentiles." In chapter 1, the first chapter of part 1, we looked at how Paul was rooted in the "traditions of [his] ancestors." Then, in chapter 4, the first chapter of part 2, we looked at how Paul's thought resembled, in some ways, other, non-Jewish thinkers within the wider Greco-Roman environment. Now, in this first chapter of part 3, it is time to see how Paul's experience of Christ led him to a new understanding of his Jewish faith, an understanding that had particular potency, both for Jews and for Gentiles, in this Greco-Roman world.

PAUL'S EXPERIENCE OF CHRIST

Paul was convinced that God had revealed Christ to him. Read Gal 1:11–16 for his narrative about his experience of the revelation of Christ:

> For I want you to know, brothers and sisters, that the gospel that was proclaimed by me is not of human origin; for I did not receive it from a human source, nor was I taught it, but I received it through a revelation of Jesus Christ.

> You have heard, no doubt, of my earlier life in Judaism. I was violently persecuting the church of God and was trying to destroy it. I advanced in Judaism beyond many among my people of the same age, for I was far more zealous for the traditions of my ancestors. But when God, who had set me apart before I was born and called me through his grace, was pleased to reveal his Son to me, so that I might proclaim him among the Gentiles, I did not confer with any human being.[1]

An Experience of Transformation

Paul tells us quite plainly that his vision of life (that is, his gospel)[2] was the result of a revelation from God. Before this revelation Paul had a different vision of life, one that he had learned and adopted as a Pharisee.[3] His commitment prior to this revelation had led him to believe that it was his duty to persecute "the church of God." Then, after an apparently sudden but certainly dramatic revelation from God, Paul reversed his position and became one of the most creative spokespersons for this church of God.

What was the nature of this experience that led Paul to reevaluate his life and his commitments? Scholars have described Paul's experience in at least three different ways: conversion, mystical experience, and call. Although there are problems with these descriptions of Paul's experience, each sheds light on an important aspect of Paul's experience.

Concerning conversion, the term frequently refers to a dramatic shift from a commitment to one religion to a commitment to a different religion. This understanding of a religious conversion, however, would hardly be a fitting description for Paul's experience, since Paul did not convert from Judaism to another religion. Rather, as a result of his experience of Christ, Paul shifted from one interpretation of Judaism (that of the Pharisees) to a new interpretation that Paul says was revealed to him by God.[4] If, however, the term *conversion* can be used in the sense that the philosophers used it—adopting a new vision of life—then one might appropriately describe Paul's experience as one that resulted in an intellectual conversion.

Paul's experience of Christ has also been described as a mystical experience.[5] To the extent that any direct experience of God or the divine is mystical, then this certainly describes Paul's experience. Paul is adamant that it was God who revealed Christ to him (Gal 1:16). He declares that Christ has "appeared" to him (1 Cor 15:8). In an unusual passage in one of his letters to the Corinthians, Paul describes an intense visionary experience (2 Cor 12:1–9). But if such ecstatic visionary experiences are the primary understanding of what constitutes mystical experience, then such a description of Paul's experience of Christ is probably not very helpful to us as we try to understand his intellectual project of articulating a vision of life. Such unusual experiences may have provided a catalyst for Paul's reinterpretation of his tradition. But it is this reinterpretation that forms the heart of what he understands to be a revelation from God. Whatever ecstatic experiences Paul may have had, his vision of life did not consist in encouraging others in a mystical life built around ecstatic

---

7:1 A Visionary Experience (2 Cor 12:2–9)

I know a man in Christ who fourteen years ago was caught up to the third heaven—whether in the body or out of the body I do not know, God knows. And I know that this man was caught up into Paradise—whether in the body or out of the body I do not know, God knows—and he heard things that cannot be told, which man may not utter. On behalf of this man I will boast, but on my own behalf I will not boast, except of my weaknesses. Though if I wish to boast, I shall not be a fool, for I shall be speaking the truth. But I refrain from it, so that no one may think more of me than he sees in me or hears from me. And to keep me from being too elated by the abundance of revelations, a thorn was given me in the flesh, a messenger of Satan, to harass me, to keep me from being too elated. Three times I besought the Lord about this, that it should leave me; but he said to me, "My grace is sufficient for you, for my power is made perfect in weakness."

---

experiences. As we shall see in the next few chapters, Paul's experience of Christ was much more socially and ethically oriented than esoterically.

Finally, Paul's experience of Christ has been described as a call to be an apostle to the Gentiles.[6] Certainly, in Paul's own description of his experience, he indicates that his apostleship was a direct result of his experience of the revelation of Christ.

> God, who had set me apart before I was born and called me through his grace, was pleased to reveal his Son to me, so that I might proclaim him among the Gentiles. (Gal 1:15–16)

But although the call to proclaim Christ among the Gentiles was the reason for the revelation, this call was not the primary content of the revelation. That is, Paul did not say that God "revealed his desire that I proclaim Christ to the Gentiles" but, rather, that God "was pleased to reveal his Son to me." According to Paul, Christ was the content of the revelation from God.

Alas, this does not tell us as much as we would like to know. But this is, perhaps, always the case when we attempt to narrate a personal experience to someone else. We simply do not have a full description[7] from Paul of what his experience was like. What we do have is Paul's extended reflections about what he understands to be the meaning of his experience for human life. We have his repeated insistence that, far from being a merely private experience for his personal benefit, Paul's experience of Christ was a revelation from God. And it is this description of Paul's experience that is the crucial one: Paul experienced Christ as the revelation of God.

A Revelation of God

You will recall that in the first chapter we learned about apocalyptic eschatology. God has promised that God will rule over the earth. For centuries Israel had thought that if it repented fully, then the promise would be fulfilled. Such was the proclamation of the prophets. But in recent centuries many in Israel had come to believe that more than Israel's repentance was needed in order for God's promise to be fulfilled. Mighty forces were at work in the world, and these forces were thwarting the fulfillment of God's promise. In apocalyptic eschatology, God's promise could only be fulfilled by the direct intervention of God. God would intervene in this

7:2 A Transforming Experience

1. Have you ever had an experience that has changed the way you thought about something? Try to describe this experience in writing. Do you think you are able to capture in words the power your experience had for you?
2. Interview someone who is older than you. Ask the person to describe one of his or her most important or unusual experiences to you. How did this experience change the person?

world and would conquer the forces that were preventing the fulfillment. The mighty force of sin and the human misperception that it generates can only be conquered by a crisis of God's intervention.

When Paul speaks of having received a revelation of God, he is drawing on the language of apocalyptic expectation. He is not interested in proclaiming some private mystical experience that he had or in sharing his religious or apostolic autobiography. His concern is, rather, to proclaim that, through Christ, God has intervened in the world and has conquered the apocalyptic force of sin that has perverted humanity's vision of God.

Like the Greco-Roman philosophers, Paul believed that humans are unable to live full and joyous lives because we misperceive reality. In short, we think about things in wrong ways. Society teaches us to value the wrong kinds of things. If we could learn to think in right ways, we would perceive the true nature of reality and the true nature of ourselves. For the philosophers, if we want to learn to think correctly, we need to go to school: We need to follow a wise teacher and start from the beginning again. Unlike the philosophers, however, Paul could not imagine that he or anyone else could simply retrain sinners to perceive correctly. God would have to reveal a new way to think. God would have to renew the minds of those who misperceive. Thus Paul says to the new believers in Rome,

Do not be conformed to this world, but be transformed by the renewal of your mind, that you may prove what is the will of God, what is good and acceptable and perfect. (Rom 12:2)

This renewal of the mind occurs through the revelation of Christ. In the following chapter we will see that this apocalyptic revelation occurred, according to Paul, in the event of the cross of Christ. That is, Paul understood the cross to be a truly apocalyptic event. It was a crisis. And through this crisis God defeated all the mighty forces that had been thwarting the fulfillment of God's promise. Through this apocalyptic event God defeated sin and rendered death impotent. Because of the apocalyptic revelation of Christ sinful humans can now perceive reality as God intends it.

A New Understanding of an Old Language

In chapter 1 we learned that Paul consistently drew on the stories and the language of Judaism in order to express his vision of human life. Paul's experience of Christ did not lead him to abandon his vocabulary or his heritage. It did, however, compel him to rethink his understanding of this heritage and to begin to use some words from Israel's vocabulary in ways that were new.[8] Indeed, much of Paul's intellectual project concerned this process of thinking through his own

7:3 Three Definitions of Righteousness

Write out the three definitions of righteousness that you learned in chapter 2.

1. _____
   _____
   _____
   _____

2. _____
   _____
   _____
   _____

3. _____
   _____
   _____
   _____

tradition in light of his experience with Christ. The chapters above on righteousness and law describe what Paul's understanding of his tradition must have been before he encountered the revelation of God in Christ. Paul does not negate what we learned in those two chapters. But he would have thought that those chapters by themselves were inadequate. In many ways, the task of the next three chapters is to describe how Paul's experience of Christ reformulated his understanding of God's righteousness. In order to prepare for our study of how Christ is the revelation of God's righteousness, it will help for you to recall the definitions of righteousness given in chapter 2.

Paul would agree with all three of these definitions of God's righteousness. His reformulation of the notion of righteousness could be described as a redistribution of the weight given to the three definitions. For the Pharisees (and for later rabbinic Judaism) the defining moment of Israel occurred at Mount Sinai when YHWH made a covenant with Israel through the mediation of Moses. Thus, for this understanding of Judaism, the second definition (righteousness as covenant faithfulness) represents the primary meaning. This understanding of righteousness highlights the figure of Moses, the priority of Israel, the central role of the law, and an understanding of justification as forgiveness and restoration to the covenant community. No one, Paul included, could deny that the heritage and the Scriptures of the Jewish people affirmed the importance of Moses, Israel, the law, or God's forgiveness.

But Paul's experience of Christ altered his understanding of righteousness. It compelled him to look at his tradition from a new perspective, and when he did, he discerned other elements preserved in this tradition, elements that had been obscured by its primary focus on a definition of God's righteousness as God's covenant faithfulness. Paul's experience of Christ led him to affirm the primary importance of its first definition: God's righteousness is God's shalom-making activity.

> ## 7:4 God Promises Salvation to All Nations
>
> Turn to me and be saved, all the ends of the earth! For I am God, and there is no other. By my-self I have sworn, from my mouth has gone forth in righteousness a word that shall not return: "To me every knee shall bow, every tongue shall swear." (Isa 45:22–23)
>
> And now the LORD says, who formed me from the womb to be his servant, to bring Jacob back to him, and that Israel might be gathered to him, for I am honored in the eyes of the LORD and my God has become my strength—he says: "It is too light a thing that you should be my ser-vant to raise up the tribes of Jacob and to restore the preserved of Israel; I will give you as a light to the nations, that my salvation may reach to the end of the earth." (Isa 49:5–6)

God's goal is to bring the entire world into right relation. This has always been God's goal. God's covenant with Israel was (and always had been) subservient to this larger vision that God had for bringing shalom to the whole cosmos. God's revelation in Christ led Paul to see that he had forgotten (or had been blinded to) God's vision for the world. God intended, and had always intended, to "peace" the world together, both Jew and Gentile. Israel's hope in the Messiah had been a hope for God's peace. But at least some in Israel had forgotten that God's peace was intended for Gentiles as well as Jews. Paul's experience of Christ consisted, in part, of God's revelation that God was including Gentiles as well as Jews in the covenant community.

This shift in Paul's perspective for understanding God's righteousness led him to articulate a new vision of human life. His presentation of God's revelation in Christ drew, in new ways, on strands of Israel's history that had been neglected in Paul's earlier Pharisaic understanding. It will be the task of the next three chapters to delineate more carefully how Paul went about weaving a new interpretation of Israel's history. For starters, however, compare the illustration below.

Illustration 10 schematizes some of the crucial differences between two competing interpretations of Israel's heritage. From Paul's standpoint, these interpretations were not simply two equally plausible options for how one might understand the history of Israel.

Illustration 10
Comparing Paul's Pharisaic and New Understandings

Paul's Pharisaic Understanding	Paul's New Understanding
Righteousness = covenant faithfulness	*Righteousness* = God's shalom-making activity
Moses as key historical figure	*Abraham* as key historical figure
Priority of Israel	*Jew and Gentile together*
Centrality of *law*	Centrality of *Christ*/Messiah
(law as wisdom of God)	(Christ as Wisdom of God)
Sin as violation of commandment	*Sin as apocalyptic power* resulting in misperception
Justification as forgiveness and restoration to community	*Justification as grace* and restoration of Creation

They represented two very different and, in Paul's mind, opposing interpretations of human life. In the one, humans seek to fulfill the law in order to secure their relationship with YHWH (covenant faithfulness). The other interpretation recognizes the apocalyptic power of sin that voids all human security, and asserts that God graciously bestows God's own righteousness upon all who trust in the Creator. Christ, in Paul's view, is the revelation of the gracious righteousness of God that will bring shalom to the entire cosmos.

CHRIST—THE REVELATION OF GOD'S RIGHTEOUSNESS

The sum of Paul's conviction lies in his assertion that in Jesus Christ the righteousness of God has been revealed. This is what Paul calls the gospel, the good news:

> But now the righteousness of God has been manifested apart from the law, although the law and the prophets bear witness to it, the righteousness of God through faith in Jesus Christ for all who believe. For there is no distinction; since all have sinned and fall short of the glory of God, they are justified by his grace as a gift, through the redemption which is in Christ Jesus, whom God put forward as an expiation by his blood, to be received by faith. This was to show God's righteousness . . . ; it was to prove at the present time that God himself is righteous and that God justifies the one who has faith in Jesus. (Rom 3:21–26)

7:5 Find the Words
In the passage quoted above, find and underline all the references to these terms—righteousness, justify, law, and sin.

These verses from Paul's Letter to the Romans present us with a limited summary of Paul's thought as I am attempting to articulate it in these chapters. It includes almost all of the key terms of Paul's theology. We have already discussed the concepts of righteousness and justification, law, sin, and death.

But there are other strange and curious terms in this text as well, and these, together with a few additions to this already formidable list, are now before us in this chapter. If we are to understand Paul's thought, we must grasp the meaning of all the key terms in this summary statement.

Imagine the complexity! For each of the last six chapters, we have concerned ourselves with one term only, or at most two. And now, with the mere invocation of the word *Christ*, we find ourselves assaulted with a panoply of new and foreign terms.[9] Indeed, the list of terms drawn from these few verses in Romans is still far from adequate to enable a full understanding of all that the term *Christ* connotes for Paul. We will also have to learn something about these terms: *Spirit, church, in Christ, resurrection,* and *Lord.* In a parody of Paul's despair over sin, we might well exclaim, Oh, who will deliver us from this confusion!

7:6 Find the New Words
1. Circle all the new words that you find in the quotation from Romans 3. How many new terms did you find?
2. How many of these did you circle: faith, believe, grace, redemption, sacrifice of atonement, by his blood, glory of God?

In the midst of all this potential confusion, there is one thing that we can state with certainty about Paul's understanding of Christ: The core of Paul's gospel resides in his conviction that Christ is the revelation of God's righteousness. This is the definition you need to commit to memory: Christ = the revelation of God's righteousness. For the purposes of our study, this means that you must not try to think of Christ as either the second person of the Trinity or even as the historical Jesus of Nazareth. Connections to these conceptualities (or actualities, if you prefer) can profitably be the focus of reflection after our study here has run its course. For now, think of *Christ* as a term that connotes a vast and complex reality for Paul. For now, *Christ* means simply this: the revelation of God's righteousness.

As you might imagine, however, this simple definition of *Christ* turns out to be quite complex. The presentation here of the complexity is formed around the three definitions of righteousness that you have just recorded (sidebar 7:3), but in reverse order.

First, we will explore God's righteousness revealed in Christ as God's justification of those estranged by sin. This will lead us into a discussion of grace and of the centrality of the cross of Christ. Second, Christ reveals God's righteousness as reconciliation, and thus as renewed covenant. Here we will explore the meaning of the term *Spirit* and how Paul envisions the new human community. And third, the overarching and determinative definition of righteousness as God's shalom-making activity is revealed in the redemption that comes to the cosmos through Christ. The sweeping nature of the redemption that is revealed through Christ will lead us to a discussion of faith and hope, the human responses to this redemption.

READING CHECK:

☑   What are the three ways in which scholars have described Paul's experience? How does Paul himself describe his experience (in Galatians 1)?

☑   How does Paul blend his apocalyptic thought with Greco-Roman concerns about the problems of human misperception?

☑   What are some of the key differences between Paul's new interpretation and the Pharisaic interpretation of Israel's past?

☑   What is the definition of Christ that you will need to remember while you read the next three chapters?

A discussion of how Christ reveals the justice and grace of God plunges into the very heart of Paul's thought. You will need to pay particular attention to three important ideas in this chapter. First, what does it mean when Paul says that "God justifies the ungodly"? Why is this a scandal? And of what does this justification consist? Second, what does Paul mean when he calls Christ "the end of the law"? And third, how does Paul use the symbol of the cross of Christ to depict his understanding of the revelation of God's righteousness?

8

Justified by Grace

"I Have Been Crucified with Christ"

At the very center of Paul's thought lies his conviction that in Christ humans become aware that God justifies sinners. This, in itself, is not startling. Paul's tradition expressed a persistent belief that God's righteousness is revealed in the many ways in which God accepts the repentant sinner back into the covenant. Remember our third definition of righteousness from chapter 2? "God's righteousness is the action of God that makes right the relationship between God and humans." When an Israelite broke the covenant, God would restore the relationship if he or she repented. But alas, Paul does not use the word *repent*. No, his message of God's righteousness is balder, more scandalous.

THE SCANDAL OF THE GOSPEL

Paul says simply this: "God justifies the ungodly" (Rom 4:5). This is the stumbling block of Paul's message, the scandal of God's revelation in Christ. God justifies the ungodly. Imagine these headlines:

GOD JUSTIFIES HITLER!

TEACHER GIVES ALL STUDENTS A'S—
REGARDLESS OF PERFORMANCE

COMPANY REWARDS ABSENTEEISM WITH
HEFTY RAISES

GOD JUSTIFIES THE UNGODLY!

This is Paul's gospel, Paul's good news. Good news? Yes, perhaps for Hitler, for lazy students, absent employees. But for the rest of us this "good news" is appalling. It is chaotic. It is anarchy. Our minds reel at the raw absurdity of the summarizing phrase, "God justifies the ungodly."

We search for sense in this statement, to find a way to bring order to this disturbing proclamation. *Christ* cannot mean this. No. We hasten to attach qualifying clauses: "God justifies the ungodly if they repent"; "God

8:1 Romans 4

What then are we to say was gained by Abraham, our ancestor according to the flesh? For if Abraham was justified by works, he has something to boast about, but not before God. For what does the scripture say? "Abraham believed God, and it was reckoned to him as righteousness." Now to one who works, wages are not reckoned as a gift but as something due. But to one who without works trusts him who justifies the ungodly, such faith is reckoned as righteousness. So also David speaks of the blessedness of those to whom God reckons righteousness apart from works: "Blessed are those whose iniquities are forgiven, and whose sins are covered; blessed is the one against whom the Lord will not reckon sin."

Is this blessedness, then, pronounced only on the circumcised, or also on the uncircumcised? We say, "Faith was reckoned to Abraham as righteousness." How then was it reckoned to him? Was it before or after he had been circumcised? It was not after, but before he was circumcised. He received the sign of circumcision as a seal of the righteousness that he had by faith while he was still uncircumcised. The purpose was to make him the ancestor of all who believe without being circumcised and who thus have righteousness reckoned to them, and likewise the ancestor of the circumcised who are not only circumcised but who also follow the example of the faith that our ancestor Abraham had before he was circumcised.

For the promise that he would inherit the world did not come to Abraham or to his descendants through the law but through the righteousness of faith. If it is the adherents of the law who are to be the heirs, faith is null and the promise is void. For the law brings wrath; but where there is no law, neither is there violation.

For this reason it depends on faith, in order that the promise may rest on grace and be guaranteed to all his descendants, not only to the adherents of the law but also to those who share the faith of Abraham (for he is the father of all of us, as it is written, "I have made you the father of many nations") — in the presence of the God in whom he believed, who gives life to the dead and calls into existence the things that do not exist. Hoping against hope, he believed that he would become "the father of many nations," according to what was said, "So numerous shall your descendants be." He did not weaken in faith when he considered his own body, which was already as good as dead (for he was about a hundred years old), or when he considered the barrenness of Sarah's womb. No distrust made him waver concerning the promise of God, but he grew strong in his faith as he gave glory to God, being fully convinced that God was able to do what he had promised. Therefore his faith "was reckoned to him as righteousness." Now the words, "it was reckoned to him," were written not for his sake alone, but for ours also. It will be reckoned to us who believe in him who raised Jesus our Lord from the dead, who was handed over to death for our trespasses and was raised for our justification.

justifies the ungodly if they are not vile"; "God justifies the ungodly if they are baptized"; "God justifies the ungodly if . . . , if . . . , *if . . .*" We want, we need qualifiers. But Paul offers none. His message leaves us raw: God justifies the ungodly.

The Example of Abraham

In Romans 4 Paul takes us only to his distant ancestor Abraham and the righteousness of God. His argument is relatively simple. It takes some of the rawness away—

but not much. We read in Genesis 15 about Abraham and God's righteousness.

> After these things the word of the LORD came to Abram in a vision, "Do not be afraid, Abram, I am your shield; your reward shall be very great." But Abram said, "O Lord GOD, what will you give me, for I continue childless, and the heir of my house is Eliezer of Damascus?" And Abram said, "You have given me no offspring, and so a slave born in my house is to be my heir." But the word of the LORD came to him, "This man shall not be your heir; no one but your very own issue shall be your heir." He brought him outside and said, "Look toward heaven and count the stars, if you are able to count them." Then he said to him, "So shall your descendants be." And he believed the LORD; and the LORD reckoned it to him as righteousness. (Gen 15:1–6)

God chooses Abraham and promises to him and his wife, Sarah, a vast progeny. Why? Because. The reason for the choice lies within the creative will of God. It is dependent on nothing else. And Abraham trusts in God's choice. As Paul says it, "No disbelief made him [Abraham] waver concerning the promise of God." Thus, Paul argues, "it was reckoned to him [Abraham] as righteousness" because Abraham was "fully convinced that God was able to do what he had promised" (Rom 4:18–22). Abraham knew God's righteousness—simply because he trusted God's creative will. No act was necessary on Abraham's part. The law had not yet been given,

not even the law in a nutshell, circumcision.[1] This is all there was: God's creative will to promise, and Abraham's trust that he, Abraham, as God's chosen partner, was more than he could possibly be.

Thus, the relationship between Abraham and God becomes for Paul the privileged paradigm of all that is necessary for righteousness. Before law, before confirmation of covenant in the flesh, there is righteousness: a surprising alchemy of will and trust, of creation and possibility. Before duty there is grace; before obedience, righteousness.

This strand of grace is not hidden in the history of Israel. It is patent. YHWH is and has always been the God of grace. "You, O YHWH, are a gracious God." God's relationship with Israel, with the human world, has always originated in God's creative will. It was not Israel who conjured up this mighty, gracious God. God has always acted first.[2] There was never anything that the people of Israel had to achieve. All was already given. God's righteousness was ever among them as gift. And the gift was radically, openly, unabashedly free.

This, then, is the meaning of the term *grace:* "free gift." As we read in Romans 3, quoted near the end of the last chapter, people "are justified by [God's] grace as a gift."

The Gift of Grace

We are justified by God's grace as a gift. But what does this mean? To say that grace is a gift is to state a redundancy. In fact, *grace*

8:2 Romans 4:18–22

In hope Abraham believed against hope, that he should become the father of many nations; as he had been told, "So shall your descendants be." He did not weaken in faith when he considered his own body, which was as good as dead because he was about a hundred years old, or when he considered the barrenness of Sarah's womb. No distrust made him waver concerning the promise of God, but he grew strong in his faith as he gave glory to God, fully convinced that God was able to do what he had promised. That is why his faith was "reckoned to him as righteousness."

means "gift." So what is this grace/gift? The answer is apparently simple: justification. But Paul poses a problem for us here. We've already seen that, as Paul states it, the gift of justification comes with no qualification—there is no mention of repentance. And therein lies the scandal of Paul's message. But another surprise is related to Paul's scandalous failure to call for repentance as a prerequisite for grace.

8:3 Which Came First?

Think about which came first—your parents' love or their rules? What does this tell you about the relationship between obedience to rules and parental love and acceptance?

In chapter 2, above, not only did we learn that repentance was an essential part of the pattern of justification that Paul had learned within Judaism; the act of justification by God consisted of God's forgiveness of the repentant sinner. But Paul does not use the term *forgiveness* as a synonym for God's grace. And that means we must be very careful at this point not to equate grace with forgiveness. God's gift of justification is not a gift of forgiveness.

Forgiveness, in Paul's tradition, is necessarily related to repentance. Thus, we are understandably scandalized by such suggestions as "God justifies Hitler," for we unconsciously translate that proclamation into "God forgives Hitler," and history surely does not record Hitler's repentance. Such a statement does, indeed, make a mockery of God's forgiveness and of genuine human repentance.

Paul's language of grace is an altogether different language from the language of re-

pentance and forgiveness. These two theological dialects, if you will, deal with different kinds of human problems. As we saw in the chapters on sin, the "solution" of forgiveness does not always work. The process of justification that we discussed in the chapter on righteousness dealt with the problem that arises when a covenant partner disobeys a commandment: If I violate the covenant and turn back to God, God will forgive me. Paul likely would have agreed wholeheartedly with this statement, as far as it goes. Paul's concern lay elsewhere, with a human difficulty that, if it is not altogether different from the problem of disobedience, nevertheless goes beyond it.

> Israel failed to attain what it sought. (Rom 11:7)

The problem Paul confronted was not that of disobedience. We might say that Paul's problem was not disobedience but rather obedience. An emendation of the above quotation can illustrate:

> Even though Israel obeyed, Israel failed to obtain what it sought.

Paul himself says something similar to this a little earlier in Romans:

> Israel who pursued righteousness which is based on law did not succeed in fulfilling that law. (Rom 9:31)

The contrast between Paul's statement of the problem and our emended form of his comment in Rom 11:7 is instructive, however. Notice that Paul uses neither the word *disobedience* nor *obedience* in his own statement. In his view, the problem is neither disobedience nor obedience (though it is manifest in both obedience and disobedience) but, rather, arises when humans attempt to define themselves in relation to the law, whether through obedience or through disobedience. This, then, is the gift of justification that Paul speaks of as grace: We are justified by God's grace "apart from the law" (Rom 3:21).

As a negation of law, grace necessarily constitutes something of a surprise in our efforts to understand Paul's thought.[3] For grace brings with it a realization that all of our careful thoughts in the preceding pages on justification, law, and sin have led us to a dead end. Grace demands that we return to the beginning and think it all through again, from another perspective.

In this, then, grace is not only a surprise (for it does not follow from the logic we have so carefully developed); it is also a scandal. For, having mastered, to some extent, the logic of the law and the logic of how sin distorts through the law, we now must toss all this hard-earned understanding overboard and begin again. I, as author, have (from the standpoint of grace) led you astray. I have taught you the logic of law and sin, only now to tell you it was all wrong. And you are right to be scandalized by this—to feel as though I have made you work hard at understanding Paul, only to be told that now you, with me, must throw this hard-won understanding aside. For grace reveals that we have misunderstood, that our logical argument in the preceding chapters has a fatal flaw.

THE END OF THE LAW

In Rom 10:4 Paul says that Christ is "the end of the law." This does not mean, of course, that the law no longer exists. We, even today, can look around us and see that law, both in the religious sense of Torah and in the legal sense of governmental or other social laws, does in fact exist. Rather, Paul means that the law is no longer the determinative element in our relation to God. God is no longer understood primarily as lawgiver.[4]

Grace takes us back to Abraham, to that originating moment of the establishment of a relationship. It locates our identity not in law (through either obedience or disobedience) but solely in the relationship to God, in God's creative will and our responsive trust.

We may succeed or fail in upholding the commandments, but our identity no longer rests upon the categories of obedience or disobedience. We no longer measure ourselves by our adherence (or failure to adhere) to the law. The law is still there, but it no longer functions as it did before. The law no longer defines. It does not define self. It does not define justification. It does not define the relationship with God. The law does not define God.

Perhaps returning to the analogy of parents and children will help clarify this notion of "the end of the law." As long as law (rules) is the primary meeting ground between parents and children (which is frequently the case especially when the children are adolescents), a free and honest relationship between parents and children is difficult, if not impossible. Teenagers sometime think that things will be better once they move out of the house and thus away from the defining strictures of their parents' rules. I am often startled at what an incredibly magic age eighteen is for adolescents; they really believe that then all this nonsense with parents will be over. They will be adults. They will be free from the law.

What many a thirty- or forty- or even sixty-year-old would say, however, is that our parents—their wishes, their words, their disapproval or approbation—still haunt us. We, even as adults, are often still unable to experience a free and honest relationship with our parents. The law is always implicitly in the background. The parents are still, at some deep level, the primary dispensers of approval, and (in our misperception) we as-

8:4 Talk to Your Parents!

Interview your parents (or another adult who is older than you) about how they relate to their own parents. To what extent do they still seek their parents' approval? To what extent do they still feel like their parents interfere in their lives?

sume that their approval is based on law. Even though we, as adults, may not admit to it openly, we still seek to please our parents; our parents' approval and pride still define success.[5]

Because of the seductive power of sin, the law becomes what determines and measures our life. And with law as the primary determinant of our identity, we extend this (parental/divine) law into all of our life. We define ourselves by how well we measure up to the expectations of others. We define others by how well they measure up to our own expectations. We live by (misperceived) law, by measurement.

Indeed, our misperception entices us to measure every aspect of our lives. Just a short sampling of questions can illustrate how pervasive this compulsive measurement is in our lives:

Are you too fat or too thin?

Are your grades good enough?

Do you make enough money?

Do you have enough friends? Are they good friends?

Do you have—or will you get—a good enough job?

Are you smart enough? funny enough? pretty enough? popular enough? rich enough? happy enough?

In short, are you good enough? Do you measure up? This question hides the real problem: How do you know what "good enough" is? What (whom) are you mea-

suring yourself against? What measurement determines your life?

The scandal of the gospel, God justifies the ungodly, ultimately lies in the fact that God justifies the ungodly apart from the law. Or to paraphrase the scandal: God accepts the ungodly without measurement. God does not measure.[6]

Now, on the one hand, this feels mighty good, for, from God's perspective, we are always enough. We do not need to measure up in order for God to accept us.[7] On the other hand, this lack of measurement requires a trust that is very hard to come by. Our identity in every area of our life has been determined by measuring up. We have defined ourselves and known ourselves by determining whether we are (or are not) good enough. But if God (our friends, our parents, our family) accepts us without measurement, then we don't ever measure up—because there is nothing to measure up to.

This, then, is the definition of grace: God justifies the ungodly—apart from the law. The Creator of life accepts us and calls us into life, neither in spite of (not measuring up) nor because of (measuring up). God accepts you just as a loving parent accepts a newborn infant, simply because you are a creature of God's creation. God accepted Abraham, neither in spite of his failures nor because of his successes, and called him to be a partner with God in righteousness.

For Paul, this discovery of a free and responsible relationship with the Creator

8:5 Measuring Identity

Check off the items below that are crucial to your identity:

1. _____gender
2. _____ethnic background
3. _____athletic ability
4. _____grades
5. _____bank account
6. _____sexual orientation
7. _____religion
8. _____appearance
9. _____popularity

Now describe yourself without referring to any of these categories. Can you do it?

was the result of his transforming experience of Christ. The grace that God revealed through Christ was the grace of justification apart from the law. One central symbol that became a potent summary, for Paul, of his new understanding of justification by grace was the cross. Through the cross of Christ God has revealed God's grace apart from the law.

THE CROSS REVEALS GOD'S GRACE

The cross is perhaps the most universally recognized symbol of Christianity. As such, it is probably both overly simple and vastly complex. It is overly simple in that it has become a simple sign of Christianity ("This is a Christian church" or "That person, who is wearing a cross, is a Christian"). As a symbol, however, the cross is complex because it has represented varying theological beliefs throughout the history of the Christian church. Fortunately for us, we do not need to trace all the variants of belief that the cross has symbolized. But unfortunately, we need to burrow beneath what is a

long history of theological interpretation in order to approach an understanding of what the first "Christian" theologian, the Apostle Paul, might have meant when he spoke about the cross of Christ.

A full exposition of what the cross meant to Paul is neither possible nor desirable within this present study. The approach will be to choose one common interpretation of the cross in Christian history and delve beneath this interpretation to another way of understanding the function of the cross in Paul's theology.

Perhaps the interpretation of the cross most frequently given in Christian history has been that it demonstrates God's (or Jesus') self-giving love. A common understanding is that Jesus' death saved us from our sins—that is, from the death that is the natural consequence of our sins. Sometimes a preacher or teacher will illustrate this view of Jesus' death by telling a story of a criminal who has been condemned to die: Someone willingly steps in and offers to take the punishment for the criminal's "sin." A "savior" gives his life in exchange for the "sinner's." A diagram of this view might look like this:

Illustration 11
A Common Understanding of Christ's Death

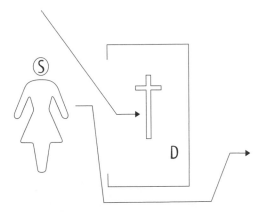

In a common understanding of the meaning of Christ's death,
we are sinners (S) who are destined to die (D). Christ (†)
intervenes and dies for us, and we are thus "free from death."

To be sure, this interpretation of the meaning of Christ's death is a powerful one. It speaks to our fear of death and our sense that we desperately want to be freed from the dire consequences of our misdeeds. But Paul's understanding of sin and death cannot support the interpretation illustrated above. In Paul's view, sin has already led us into death. We already experience the alienation and enslavement that are the results of our participation in sin. Our struggles with autonomy and heteronomy have already mired us in the impossible situation that Paul describes as death. The above illustration, then, no matter how powerful, does not suffice to explain Paul's understanding of the cross of Christ.

The Cross as Symbol

As we learned in the last chapter, Paul's vision of life was the result of what he believed to be a revelation from God. Something transformed Paul's life and thought. In the Letter to the Galatians, Paul describes this transformation by using the language of crucifixion. Paul had not been present at the crucifixion of Jesus. Certainly he was not historically "crucified with Christ." And yet Paul confidently uses the language of co-crucifixion to describe his experience of transformation upon receiving a revelation from God. The cross, then, is for Paul both history and symbol. The symbolic power of the cross depends upon the historical fact that the man Jesus of Nazareth was crucified

---

8:6 What Paul Says about the Cross

For through the law I died to the law, so that I might live to God. I have been crucified with Christ; and it is no longer I who live, but it is Christ who lives in me. And the life I now live in the flesh I live by faith in the Son of God, who loved me and gave himself for me. (Gal 2:19–20)

May I never boast of anything except the cross of our Lord Jesus Christ, by which the world has been crucified to me, and I to the world. For neither circumcision nor uncircumcision is anything; but a new creation is everything! (Gal 6:14–15)

For the message about the cross is foolishness to those who are perishing, but to us who are being saved it is the power of God. For it is written, "I will destroy the wisdom of the wise, and the discernment of the discerning I will thwart." Where is the one who is wise? Where is the scribe? Where is the debater of this age? Has not God made foolish the wisdom of the world? For since, in the wisdom of God, the world did not know God through wisdom, God decided, through the foolishness of our proclamation, to save those who believe. For Jews demand signs and Greeks desire wisdom, but we proclaim Christ crucified, a stumbling block to Jews and foolishness to Gentiles, but to those who are the called, both Jews and Greeks, Christ the power of God and the wisdom of God. For God's foolishness is wiser than human wisdom, and God's weakness is stronger than human strength. (1 Cor 1:18–25)

on a Roman cross. But our remembrance of this historic event is, in some ways, dependent upon the potent ways in which Paul the apostle claimed this historic occurrence as a controlling metaphor to describe his own experience of transformation.

Paul did not believe that his experience of transformation was simply a random event in his own personal life. When he calls this experience a revelation of God, he makes clear that his own experience has a connection to something that, at least in Paul's view, is ultimately true about human life. This was not simply a revelation about Paul's psychological well-being or about his future. The revelation of God that transformed Paul's life was a revelation that concerned the truth about all human life. Paul uses the cross as a potent symbol for this truth. The cross becomes a metaphor not just for Paul's own experience of having died to an old world and living in a "new creation" but for how humans experience the grace of God.

Christ Died

First, the cross symbolizes the judgment of God on the world of sin and death and the human experience of dying to that old world. The logic of the law is inescapable. It inhabits (or invades) every nook and cranny of our lives. It makes life manageable because it allows us to measure things and to anticipate outcomes. It helps us make decisions because its very logic enables us to predict the results of our actions. But the cross explodes the inherent predictability of law.

The cross gives the lie to our expectations that we, through the law, can control our own life and its outcomes. The cross is first a symbol of the reality of death. According to any human measurement, the crucifixion of Jesus was a demonstration of failure. Death is failure; it is the end of life. It is loss. It is irremediable. As we saw in the chapters on sin, our knowledge of the law does not lead us to life. It does not enable us to make wise choices or achieve plausible outcomes. Our human aspirations are not fulfilled. We are thwarted, not only by our circumstances and the people around us but even by our own drives and misperceptions. Life is not fair. Things don't balance out. And none of us can anticipate either the trials or the achievements that lie in our futures. We can plan for them. We can anticipate them. But we cannot ensure them. And at the end of all this careful effort lies, for each of us, only death. The cross reveals the inescapability of the ultimate impotence of all human efforts to control life. We do, in

---

8:7 Thinking about Death

Death is a difficult subject to think about, but in order to grasp the depth of Paul's understanding of Christ, it is necessary for us to think about death and what death means. Perhaps the following questions will help . . .

1. How have you encountered death? What close friends or family members have died?
2. How did/do you respond to these deaths?
3. Do you believe that their deaths impoverished their impact on your life?
4. Do you believe that their love for you or yours for them is gone now that they are dead?
5. In what ways, then, is death an end to their lives?
6. Without invoking notions of an afterlife or heaven, in what ways is death not an end to their lives?

fact, all die. Even forgiveness does not occlude this ultimate outcome. Our scars remain. Death is certain.

This is the first aspect of the revelation of the cross. In it Paul saw revealed the depth of the pain and the impotence, the hurt and the impossibility of human life. In the cross God has displayed God's judgment against the power of sin, which has seduced humans into the presumption that we can control life. All the pain of the scars that are left after repentance and forgiveness have done their work finds full display in the excruciating death of Jesus of Nazareth. "Yes," Paul says, "life is like that."

The power of the cross is that it symbolizes our own inevitable deaths. But the symbol is larger than just a reference to our experience of futility. The cross demonstrates, according to Paul, that Jesus, one sent by the God of Israel, has joined us at our deepest vulnerability. Christ has experienced death with us. Christ has entered our futility and shares with us the common fate of all humanity.

Illustration 12
Paul's Understanding of Christ's Death

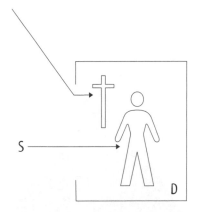

In Paul's understanding of the meaning of Christ's death, we are sinners (S) who have already entered death (D). Christ (†) joins us in our death and dies with us.

The Cross Shatters Our Misperception

But the cross is not just a revelation of the violent impotency of human life, of the hopelessness inherent in all human measurement. Paul also sees the cross as revelatory of a new perception of God, and therefore of a new kind of life, a life not based on measurement. For it is through the cross that God reveals that God is a God of grace, not a God with a measuring stick. Our conviction that God (our parents, our friends, our loved ones) measures us keeps us from recognizing the pure grace of love. Even our pious insistence that God is a God of forgiveness can conspire to trap us in this old world. For such a God of forgiveness is one who forgives us when we acknowledge that we don't measure up. We still misperceive such a God as primarily concerned about measurement. We fail to see God's grace.

Because we are mired in our misperception of the creator's good intent, the good news of God's grace must come to us as a surprise of revelation. In Paul's experience, it is an encounter with Christ that reveals to us the good news of God's grace. Christ reveals and mediates God's grace to us, shattering our misperception and enabling us to recognize and fulfill God's good intention for us. How does Christ mediate God's grace?

In a college where I formerly taught, we had a course that all the senior majors and minors in our department were required to take. In it the students each write several drafts of a major paper and submit each draft to every other student as well as to the professor for comments and critique. What happens far too often is that the students simply accept the critique (especially the professor's critique) and attempt, in their next draft, to fix the problem. They seem somehow afraid to reject or modify any of the critique, feeling compelled to fix everything so that their

next draft will measure up to their percep-
tions of the professor's expectations. As a
result, each succeeding draft can be more
convoluted than the last. The students need
to have more self-confidence about discerning what advice is useful and what advice is
not useful, and about how to use the advice
in ways that will help the overall project. But
such discernment takes courage, and, where
grades (measurement) are concerned, such
courage is difficult to come by indeed.

Thus, whether the advice is rejected or
uncritically accepted, the advice results in
creating a worse situation. As long as the advice is misperceived, as long as the intention
of the adviser is misperceived, no advice
can help. The adviser can do nothing to convince the advisee that his or her perception is
inaccurate.

The startling aspect of the illusion of the
"bird in the bush" is that when we first read
it, we have no doubt that we are reading it
correctly. Indeed, we can (mis)read it repeat-
edly and still not see that we are reading it in-
correctly. This is why misperception is such a
pernicious problem. We do not know that
we are misperceiving. In fact, once we see
that we have been misperceiving, then we no
longer misperceive.

Something new must happen before the
advice can be accepted. It often happens, for
example, that another professor in the department is able to work with a student in
order to encourage the student to evaluate
the various critiques. This professor can, perhaps, alleviate the student's fear that the
course professor will flunk her if she doesn't
do exactly what the professor wants her to
do. Through this third party (who has no authority of assigning a final grade) the student
may come to relate to the course professor's
critique not as law but as helpful counsel.
These critiques can now be seen as suggestions that can help her to write a better
paper. The third party can encourage her to

Illustration 13
What's Wrong with these Drawings?

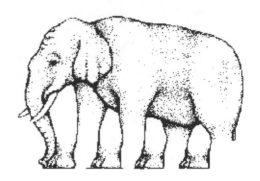

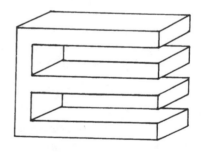

> ### 8:8 Pleasing God—Pleasing Our Parents
>
> One of the ironies of sin's power is that it seduces us into thinking about good things in destructive ways. For instance, reflect on the following questions:
>
> 1. Do you think it is good to want to please God?
> 2. Do you think it is good to want to please your parents?
> 3. Do you think it is good to live your life in order to please God?
> 4. Do you think it is good to live your life in order to please your parents?
> 5. Do you think God wants you to live your life primarily in order to please God?
> 6. Do you think your parents want you to live your life primarily in order to please them?
>
> What do you learn about life, about your parents' desires for you, and about your view of God from answering these questions?

use the critiques to help her write her own paper (rather than the professor's). This is, after all, what the course professor wants for the student, that she write her own paper, and that it be a good paper.

Through this third party the student is able to forget her own perception momentarily. She is "freed from the law" and thus becomes able to respond more genuinely, more actively to the critiques of the course professor. Through the other professor the student is able to perceive her own misperception. The course professor is not against her; neither is he telling her what to do in order to get a good grade, in order to please him. The goal of the professor all along has been to mentor the student in how to write a superior paper. The professor still retains all authority, but the student's understanding of this authority, and thus her response to it, has been radically altered. Through the student's active engagement with this third party, the student comes to see that the course professor is on her side.

For Paul, Christ is this third party who is able to free us from our misperception of God. Through him who has shared in our vulnerability and despair, we are able to perceive our own misperception. We recognize that Christ is there for us. Through him God's intention and our perception become one. Christ is the revelation of the true God, a God who, all along, has been on our side. A new understanding of authority emerges. Where law reigns, God's authority is enforced by measurement. We accede (either willingly or rebelliously) to that authority through submitting to or resisting that measurement. But according to Paul, law no longer reigns. God's authority resides not in law but in loving grace, not in measurement but in mentoring.

CONCLUSION

Thus does the cross reconcile us to God, to ourselves. We have seen in the last section that Paul uses the symbol of the cross to depict his confidence about a new perception of God. The cross, displaying as it does the extreme of human measurement, has revealed the ultimate folly of a life that finds its identity through measurement, of achievement, honor, and the false security that such measurements offer. The cross, by revealing the emptiness of human vision as perverted by sin, reveals that the God who has created us, the God who calls us, is not a God-against-us but is in truth a God-for-us. God is One who loves with a creative power that knows no limits, that defies all human measurings. Rather than being a God with a measuring stick, a God who circumscribes human space and demands adherence to preordained standards, God revels in that daringly open space of creative love and un-measurable trust.

READING CHECK:

☑ Why is it a scandal to suggest that God justifies the ungodly?

☑ Describe how Paul uses Abraham as an example of human faith and God's righteousness.

☑ How is Christ the end of the law?

☑ Describe what the cross reveals about God and about humanity.

In this chapter you will discover that the revelation of God in Christ reconciles Jews and Gentiles and also has practical consequences for how humans live together in community. First, the Spirit of God provides the basis for a common moral life. Second, God's Spirit enables us to express our unique individuality. And third, the Spirit of God makes possible a new understanding of human community. By the end of this chapter, you should be able to articulate how living "according to the Spirit" enables human life.

9

Spirit and Community

"One Body in Christ"

A RECONCILIATION

Paul's conviction that in Christ humans were justified apart from the law had far-reaching implications for his understanding of human life in general and of Judaism in particular. In Paul's Pharisaic Jewish tradition, the law was the centerpiece of how one thought not only about God but also about human community. The law, as we learned in chapter 3, was God's gracious gift to the people of Israel. Through the centuries this law had, for many Jews, come to define the essence of what it meant to be a Jew. The three practices of circumcision, dietary regulations, and Sabbath observance served as clear external signs of Jewish adherence to the law. These practices marked the Jews off as a peculiar people among the nations. The law was given so that Israel would know how to participate with YHWH in bringing shalom to the world. But this very law, which

had the ultimate goal of bringing peace to all peoples, had become the dividing line between Israel and other nations.

Paul's assertion that in Christ God justifies sinners apart from the law affects, then, not only his understanding of how God makes right the relationship between God and humans;[1] it also affects his understanding of God's righteousness as faithfulness to a covenant with Israel.[2] God had called Israel to be God's partner in bringing shalom to the world. And now, through Christ, this shalom has become a reality. In Christ, God has justified the ungodly. This justification of the sinner apart from the law has brought about a reconciliation of sinners to their Creator (see 2 Cor 5:16–21). But such a reconciliation of humans to their Creator also accomplishes, in Paul's view, a reconciliation of humans among themselves. An early student of Paul's said it this way:

But now in Christ Jesus you [Gentiles] who once were far off have been brought near by the blood of Christ. For he is our peace; in his flesh he has made both groups [Jews and Gentiles] into one and has broken down the dividing wall, that is, the hostility between us. He has abolished the law with its commandments and ordinances, that he might create in himself one new humanity in place of the two, thus making peace, and might reconcile both groups to God in one body through the cross, thus putting to death that hostility through it. So he came and proclaimed peace to you who were far off and peace to those who were near; for through him both of us have access in one Spirit to the Father. (Eph 2:13–18)[3]

This reconciliation between Jews and Gentiles was a central concern of Paul's life and ministry.[4] He was adamant that the revelation of God in Christ necessitated a new understanding of the relationship between Jews and Gentiles. God justifies sinners apart from the law. How, then, could circumcision, the chief symbol of commitment to law, function as the initiation rite into the community of those who were justified by and who lived by God's grace? Along with other early followers of Jesus, Paul adopted baptism as the appropriate initiation rite into the community:

As many of you as were baptized into Christ have clothed yourselves with Christ. There is no longer Jew or Greek, there is no longer slave or free, there is no longer male and female; for all of you are one in Christ Jesus. (Gal 3:27–28)

The rite of baptism, in Paul's understanding, replaces that of circumcision. Whereas circumcision resulted in a clear demarcation between Jews and Gentiles, in baptism such ethnic (and social and gender) distinctions are rendered insignificant. The grace of God in Christ Jesus reconciles humans and brings them into a new community.

But if this new community has come into being apart from the law, by what means are the members of this community to know how to be effective community members? The law had been given so that Israel would know how to be an effective partner with YHWH in bringing shalom to the world. Will not the demotion of law from its place of centrality mean that this new community flounders in its own efforts to be an effective partner with YHWH? Not so, according to Paul, for the Spirit of God will inform the community in its members' relations with each other and with the world.

A COMMON MORAL LIFE

Paul believed that the cross revealed that we are reconciled to a God who justifies sinners apart from the law. God's love defies measurement. Through Christ humans are reconciled to being creatures of this boundless God who does not measure. Not having to create ourselves, we are finally free to be simply human. No longer are we primarily identified by ethnicity, gender, or socioeconomic status. We are first and foremost creatures of God. Thus reconciled to a boundless and loving creator, we are finally able to see ourselves as we are. That is, to see ourselves, and each other, from the perspective of God.

And what do we look like from the perspective of God? We look like humans. Humans whom God loves. Humans whom God created. Humans whom God has no need to measure. We are finally free to be simply human.[5] You will remember that Paul, while he never disparages human nature, nevertheless ascribes sin to that human propensity to live "according to the flesh." That is, when we humans live according to our own limited vision of what it means to be human, we always, necessarily, mess things up—because we simply cannot see the whole picture. We always distort, limit, overdo, underdo. But when we live according to God's vision of what it means to be human, when we trust God's revelation in Christ, then Paul says we are living "according to the Spirit."

The antithesis between living according to the flesh and living according to the Spirit has led many people to believe that Paul is opposed to the physical and in favor of the spiritual. Many interpreters of Paul have, indeed, argued that Paul is a mystic or a spiritualist. But such a reading of Paul disregards the very here-and-now, this-wordly impact of Paul's understanding. Look at the following passage, where Paul discusses the contrast between living according to the flesh and living according to the Spirit:

> Live by the Spirit, I say, and do not gratify the desires of the flesh. For what the flesh desires is opposed to the Spirit, and what the Spirit desires is opposed to the flesh; for these are opposed to each other, to prevent you from doing what you want. But if you are led by the Spirit, you are not subject to the law. Now the works of the flesh are obvious: fornication, impurity, licentiousness, idolatry, sorcery, enmities, strife, jealousy, anger, quarrels, dissensions, factions, envy, drunkenness, carousing, and things like these. I am warning, as I warned you before: those who do such things will not inherit the kingdom of God.
>
> By contrast, the fruit of the Spirit is love, joy, peace, patience, kindness, generosity, faithfulness, gentleness, and self-control. There is no law against such things. And those who belong to Christ Jesus have crucified the flesh with its passions and desires. If we live by the Spirit, let us also be guided by the Spirit. (Gal 5:16–25)

It should be clear from this passage that Paul understands *flesh* and *Spirit* as antonyms. These terms designate two opposite ways of living in the world.

9:1 Spirit Versus Flesh

In light of Galatians 5, compare the characteristics of living according to the Spirit and living according to the flesh.

Notice that the terms in Galatians 5 have to do with how we live together in this human world: Either we relate to one another in jealous, angry, or contentious ways or we do so in loving, patient, and generous ways. When we perceive our lives together from the perspective of God, as revealed in Christ, we are able to live the best of human lives. It is our own misperception of ourselves, of others, and of our Creator (living according to the flesh) that traps us into living lives that might well be described as being less than human. In the simplest of terms, living according to the flesh is equivalent to living an immoral and inhumane life; living according to the Spirit is equivalent to living a humane and moral life.

In this passage from Galatians Paul can help us understand the connection between Christ and living according to the Spirit. We learned in the last chapter that Christ reveals God's righteousness apart from the law.

9:2 Spirit and Law

What two things does Paul have to say in the Galatians passage about the relationship between law and living according to the Spirit?

Again, in Galatians 5 Paul seems to be somewhat double-minded about the law.[6] First he seems to reject the law by saying that those who are led by the Spirit "are not subject to the law." Then he emphasizes that "there is no law against" living according to the Spirit. Thus, Paul's position could not be described as antinomian,[7] for those who are led by the Spirit do not live in any way that is against the law. Indeed, their lives are in full accordance with the law. And yet it is not because of the law that Spirit-led people live in accordance with the law.

Some years ago, I opened my home to a foster daughter for a short period of time. Since she was a ward of the state, I had to fill out a considerable amount of paperwork before the county would allow her to remain in my home. I was disconcerted by one of these papers in particular. I was required to sign a paper saying that if my foster daughter had a paying job, I would not take her money away from her. In short, I had to sign a paper that said I would not steal her money. I needed no "law" to tell me that I shouldn't do that. In fact, it is difficult (and naive) for me to believe that anyone would need to sign a paper saying he or she wouldn't steal from a foster child. I did not steal her money during the year she lived with me, but it was not because of this piece of paper that I didn't steal. It was because I had no desire to steal from her. Thus, I lived in accordance with the law, although I did not do so because of the law.

God's righteousness has always been a righteousness apart from the law, according to Paul. That is, God's righteousness, God's passionate activity in bringing shalom to this created world, existed before the law. The law reflects this righteousness. It describes this righteousness. It helps humans know what righteousness looks like. But it cannot bring about this righteousness. Indeed, because of the convoluted ways in which sin perverts human perception of the law and diverts our attention from God to the law, the law seduces us into action that is against the law.[8]

But those who have experienced the shattering of human misperception through the revelation of the cross of Christ now see themselves and other humans from the perspective of God. The "Spirit of God" lives in them (see Rom 8:9), and living by this Spirit rather than with distorted human perception, they experience the righteousness of God that has always been apart from the law.

Something about this view is troubling, however. If, in order to live a fully humane life in this world, we each have to be filled by the Spirit of some God, will we not be simply some sort of automatons, with no individual wills or personalities? If we see each other as equal creatures of God, does that not mean that there are no differentiations among us, that we are all alike? Do the categories of Jew and Gentile, female and male, no longer have any meaning at all? We may be reconciled to each other and to God, but who would want a reconciliation that made us all the same—do the same, think the same, be the same? It sounds pretty boring and frightfully oppressive.

9:3 Obedience from the Heart

1. Can you think of examples where you have done the right thing not because you were "following the law" or trying to do the "right thing" but simply because it seemed the obvious way to relate to another person?
2. Can you think of times when someone has surprised you by thanking you for something that you did? That is, you were surprised that what you did was special; you thought everyone acted that way.

A DIVERSE COMMUNITY

Fortunately, as we read other passages where Paul talks about the Spirit, we see that this is precisely not what Paul envisions. Here is what Paul says about the Spirit in his First Letter to the Corinthians:

> To each is given the manifestation of the Spirit for the common good. To one is given through the Spirit the utterance of wisdom, and to another the utterance of knowledge according to the same Spirit, to another faith by the same Spirit, to another gifts of healing by the one Spirit, to another the working of miracles, to another prophecy, to another the discernment of spirits, to another various kinds of tongues, to another the interpretation of tongues. All these are activated by one and the same Spirit, who allots to each one individually just as the Spirit chooses. (1 Cor 12:7–11)

The presence of the Spirit in human lives is evidenced not only in a common moral life. It is this same Spirit that inspires the power of human individuality. The Spirit activates distinct abilities within individual humans. Paul called these abilities *charismata,* or "spiritual gifts." The grace *(charis)* of Christ unlooses in us, as it were, particular human abilities. See the list of spiritual gifts that Paul enumerates in his Letter to the Romans:

> We have gifts that differ according to the grace given to us: prophecy, in proportion to faith; ministry, in ministering; the teacher, in teaching; the exhorter, in exhortation; the giver, in generosity; the leader, in diligence; the compassionate, in cheerfulness. (Rom 12:6–8)

Those who live their lives according to the Spirit, then, are not all the same. In Paul's view, it is precisely the Spirit that enables humans to express their own individuality, and to do so with strength. In fact, it is the presence of law, inasmuch as it en-

tices us to measure ourselves and others, that can (and often does) create such rigid standards within a community that everyone is required to be the same in order to measure up.

In order to understand how the Spirit works to bring about a diverse community, we need to go back to what we learned in the chapters on sin. We learned that there are two approaches to the law, both of which lead to death. The autonomous reaction to law arises because we refuse to allow the law to define who we are. We want to be individuals, to determine our own measurement. The heteronomous reaction to the law arises because we want to measure up to the standards that others have set for us. In neither case are we truly free to be ourselves, for the autonomous person nevertheless measures himself over against the law of another, and the heteronomous person measures herself in order to "be someone." In neither case is it simply okay to be who or what we are apart from the law.

Christ reveals, however, that in fact God has always loved us apart from the law. God created us in love. God says we are okay. This fundamental affirmation of God occurred long before any law arrived. Does it mean we're perfect? Does it mean that we measure up to God's standards? Ah, but "measuring up" language is our human way of looking at things. It's not the way God talks. It's not the way God thinks about human life. If God creates each of us as unique human beings, then what would "perfect" be, anyway? Would it not demean the creativity of God to presume that God wanted us all to measure up to some ideal standard? What God most wants is for us to be free to be the creatures God created. And that means that we are creatures with limits.

It is an important lesson to learn: Every strength is the flip side of a weakness; and every weakness is the flip side of a strength. A

9:4 Positives into Negatives

See how you do at thinking through the flip sides of the following characteristics. In column A: What are some negatives about these strengths? How can these strengths express themselves in negative ways? In column B: How might these weaknesses be transformed into strengths? The first one in each column is done for you as an example:

COLUMN A

confident _____*arrogant*_____

intelligent _____

leader _____

dramatic _____

humorous_____

organized_____

responsible_____

sensitive _____

COLUMN B

nosy _____*curious*_____

bossy_____

rebellious_____

shy _____

childish _____

egocentric _____

boring _____

spendthrift_____

person who is shy is not likely ever to have to apologize for saying something brash. Which is worse? Which is better? To be shy or to speak out of place? How would we measure such a thing? Shy people are limited. Of course! Brash people are limited. Of course! But who ever said humans weren't limited? It's the way we were created. God never intended it to be otherwise.

Does this mean, however, that we should just accept our limitations and not try to improve ourselves, to progress and expand our abilities? One strong counter to Paul's teaching of grace has always been that it seems too easy. The free gift of grace might, some say, seduce us into laziness. The claim that we are fully accepted by God just as we are might be nothing more than a blind acceptance of the status quo. Like the alcoholic who declares that alcoholism is a disease and thus finds an excuse to keep on drinking, is it not irresponsible simply to declare, "This is just the way I am"?

And yet, if we look at the story that alcoholics tell of themselves, we find that this is rarely what happens. In fact, the declaration "I am an alcoholic" is a courageous moment of truth telling. Frequently such a declaration is the prelude to recovery. Knowing that I am limited (e.g., by alcoholism), I can take appropriate steps to keep this limitation from destroying my life. I no longer need to hide from others. I am willing to let others help me. So it is with the Spirit of God, according to Paul. By the grace of God, I come to full recognition of who I am and of my human limitations. I accept myself because God has accepted me, warts and all, so to speak. This acceptance yields clear vision about myself and my world. I no longer need to organize my life around trying to ignore or shore up my limitations. I no longer need to deny my limitations or hide them from myself or others. Granting my own limitations, I am free to focus on living fruitfully within them. It is, according to Paul, the spiritual gifts that allow us to live fruitfully, bearing both the fruits of right relationships with other humans and the fruits of building up those around us. Through the spiritual gifts we finally fit into the world, using both our gifts and our limitations in ways that contribute to the larger community.

The Spirit of the One who created us activates within us spiritual gifts *(charismata),* the positive aspects of our human personalities, while freeing us from feeling as though we have to have every conceivable positive human character trait:

- There will be some people who, led by the Spirit, will have the particular gift of organization—but these people will probably not be wildly creative free spirits.

- There will be some people who, led by the Spirit, will be extravagantly generous with their money—but these people may not be the best folks to serve as the treasurers of an organization.

- There will be some people who, led by the Spirit, will be amazingly sensitive to the needs and hurts of the people around them—but these people will likely not be able to make the difficult decision to lead a group in a direction that will necessarily cause some pain.

When humans live their lives according to the flesh, the problem is not primarily that we are unable to measure up.[9] The more serious problem, according to Paul, is that the very thing that could be our strength has become our Achilles' heel. If we relate this to what we've learned about sin, we could say that the desire to be an autonomous self is not in any way a bad or wrong desire. There is nothing wrong with wanting to be an individual. It is, in fact, a good, and we might even say a God-given, desire. The problem is that because of our misperception of God and ourselves, this good desire has led us into a place that we never wanted to be, into alien-

ation from God, our parents, our society. Similarly, the heteronomous desire to please God (our parents, our friends, our teachers) is in no way a bad or wrong desire. There is nothing wrong with wanting to please others. It is a joyous and wonderful thing to please God, to be a pleasure to our parents and our friends. The problem is that, again, because of our misperception of God and ourselves, this good desire has led us into a situation where we no longer know who we are.

The grace that comes through Christ is not some sort of removal of the bad parts of us, for the very things that have destroyed us are our greatest assets—the desire to be a self, the desire to please others. Rather, the grace *(charis)* that comes through Christ, according to Paul, activates these good parts of who we are (the spiritual gifts, the *charismata)* in such ways that they no longer destroy us. Free to be a self, as God has always intended, we no longer have to fight for the right to be ourselves and thus alienate ourselves from God or others. Free to be a pleasure to God, we no longer have to efface ourselves in order to earn God's pleasure.

This view of Paul's, that God's Spirit frees us to be the loved and limited humans that God created us to be, is, to some extent, different from other views of humanity in the ancient world. On the whole, the Greek philosophers defined human behavior according to some notion of the ideal human. Aristotle's view (which was accepted by many) was that the ideal human would find the perfect mean between two opposites. So, for instance, it was not ideal to be totally brave or totally cowardly. Someone who was too brave would be foolhardy; and cowardliness is a vice by anyone's standards. The ideal human will have the right mix of bravery and cowardliness.

The goal was to find what may be called the Aristotelian mean between these sets of opposites. We meet this view today when we talk about being well balanced, neither too

9:5 The Aristotelian Mean

First, in feelings of fear and confidence the mean is bravery. . . . In pleasure and pains . . . the mean is temperance and the excess intemperance. . . . In giving and taking money the mean is generosity, the excess wastefulness and the deficiency ungenerosity. . . . In honour and dishonour the mean is magnanimity, the excess something called a sort of vanity, and the deficiency pusillanimity. . . . In truth-telling, then, let us call the intermediate person truthful, and the mean truthfulness; pretence that overstates will be boastfulness, and the person who has it boastful; pretence that understates will be self-deprecation, and the person who has it self-deprecating. Hence it is hard work to be excellent, since in each case it is hard work to find what is intermediate; e.g., not everyone, but only one who knows, finds the midpoint in a circle. So also getting angry, or giving and spending money, is easy and anyone can do it; but doing it to the right person, in the right amount, at the right time, for the right end, and in the right way is no longer easy, nor can everyone do it. (Aristotle, Nicomachean Ethics 2.3, Irwin)[10]

shy nor too brash; neither too rigid nor too freewheeling; neither too emotional nor overly rational. It requires much practice, much maturity, and much concentration and effort to arrive at this ideal mean.

Paul's view was very different from this. He would not say, for instance, that by the infusion of some divine Spirit, humans would automatically or magically express some ideal standard of human conduct.[11] He had a different way of conceiving things altogether. Paul had no notion of an ideal human. He did, however, have a utopian vision of an ideal human community.

"YOU ARE THE BODY OF CHRIST"

One of the images that Paul uses to describe how an ideal human community functions is that of the human body. See, for example, what he says to the community at Corinth:

For just as the body is one and has many members, and all the members of the body, though many, are one body, so it is with Christ. For by one Spirit we were all baptized into one body—Jews or Greeks, slaves or free—and all were made to drink of one Spirit.

For the body does not consist of one member but of many. If the foot should say, "Because I am not a hand, I do not belong to the body," that would not make it any less a part of the body. And if the ear should say, "Because I am not an eye, I do not belong to the body," that would not make it any less a part of the body. If the whole body were an eye, where would be the hearing? If the whole body were an ear, where would be the sense of smell? But as it is, God arranged the organs in the body, each one of them as God chose. If all were a single organ, where would the body be? As it is, there are many parts, yet one body. The eye cannot say to the hand, "I have no need of you," nor again the head to the feet, "I have no need of you." On the contrary, the parts of the body which seem to be weaker are indispensable, and those parts of the body which we think less honorable we invest with greater modesty, which our more presentable parts do not require. But God has so adjusted the body, giving the greater honor to the inferior part, that there may be no discord in the body, but that the members may have the same care for one another. If one member suffers, all suffer together; if one member is honored, all rejoice together.

Now you are the body of Christ and individually members of it. (1 Cor 12:12–27)

9:6 Eye-Hand Coordination

1. In what ways do you make your strongest contribution to a group? How might it free you to understand that you didn't have to "be everything"? Can you identify the strengths of others in your group? How might recognizing their unique strengths enable you to support them better in their participation in the group?
2. What kinds of strengths do others in the group need to have in order for your strengths to be most effective?

Given Paul's Jewish heritage, it is not surprising that he would express such a strong belief in the primary value of community. Do you remember the illustrations we used in the chapter on law about the athletic team or the orchestra? The description that Paul gives here in 1 Corinthians about the "body of Christ" fits well with what we discussed about how Israel understood its obedience to the law as a joint obedience. The goal is not primarily to be an ideal eye or an ideal hand. Rather, the goal is that the body function well together, to have "ideal eye-hand coordination," we might say.

This body is a metaphor for Paul's notion of the ideal human community. What community is that? Well, it is the body of Christ. Do you remember the definition of *Christ* that you were asked to commit to memory at the end of chapter 7? In the space below, replace the word *Christ* with this definition and see what you get.

Thus, the ideal human community, in Paul's view, is the community that reveals the righteousness of God. It is the community that participates with God in God's passionate activity to bring shalom to this created world. Through Christ, according to Paul, we are enabled to be covenant partners with God. This brings us back full circle to the chapter on righteousness, where we learned that God's righteousness is God's covenant faithfulness.

What, then, is the difference between Paul's view of the church as the ideal human community and the covenant between God and Israel as it was established at Sinai? The difference is not so much an alteration of the view presented in chapter 2; it is more a logical extension (at least in Paul's mind) of this understanding of God's covenant with Israel. In order to pursue this question, however, we will need to discuss how Christ revealed the redemption that God's righteousness brings to the cosmos.

9:7 Definition of "Body of Christ"

Christ = _____

_____

_____

Therefore, the body of Christ = _____

_____

_____

READING CHECK:

☑ How does Paul's view that righteousness comes "apart from the law" affect the relations between Jews and Gentiles?

☑ Describe the life that is led according to the Spirit. How is this life related to the law?

☑ What are charismata, and how are they related to charis?

☑ How is Paul's view of the charismata different from Aristotle's view of the virtues?

☑ Why does Paul not hold to a vision of an ideal human?

*t*his final chapter will bring us back to the beginning of our study. We learned in chapter 2 that God's righteousness was God's shalom-making activity. In the previous two chapters we have looked at how Paul interpreted the revelation of God in Christ as revealing new ways of understanding ourselves and other humans. It is crucial to an understanding of Paul's overall thought, however, to see that this new perception of our humanity is related to a new vision of the entire cosmos. God's shalom is not yet complete. The full revelation of Christ (as God's righteousness) lies in the future. In the first major section of this chapter, you will learn about the language of resurrection and exaltation, a language that expresses a confidence in God's ultimate shalom. At the end of this chapter, you should be able to define faith and explain the importance of hope as the believers await the full shalom of God.

10

Faith and Hope

"Jesus Christ Is Lord"

In 1 Corinthians 15 Paul quotes one of the earliest creeds of the Christian church. This is what the early "Nazarenes" proclaimed about this Jesus whom they called the Messiah (= Christ):

> Christ died for our sins in accordance with
>   the Scriptures
>   and he was buried;
>
> Christ was raised on the third day in
>   accordance with the Scriptures,
>   and he appeared to Cephas and then to
>   the twelve. (1 Cor 15:3–5)

This short creed[1] is one of several examples of material that Paul received from the early believers in Jesus. That is, Paul drew not only on his Jewish heritage and the Greco-Roman milieu; after his experience of Christ, he also adopted and adapted the language and thought of other early believers in Jesus. Central to this early Christian material that Paul quotes in his letters are two related

claims. First, the early believers in Jesus professed that "God has raised this Jesus (Christ) from the dead" and that as a result of God's action, "Jesus Christ is Lord" (Rom 10:9).

You may have thought it odd that in chapter 8, above, when we looked at how Paul interpreted Christ's crucifixion, there was no mention of the resurrection. No doubt the early believers in Jesus would have been astonished that anyone could speak of the cross of Christ without also mentioning either Christ's resurrection or his lordship. As the creed of 1 Corinthians illustrates, the death and resurrection of Christ belong together.

But twenty centuries separate us from those early years. We today too easily leap from death to resurrection, for (whether Christian or not) we have heard the story all of our lives. And this very familiarity with the story keeps us from taking the death seriously (he was, after all, only dead for a short time, not really dead in the way our family and our friends die); it also seduces us into a serious failure to understand the meaning of resurrection. Because we know the story—"After three days he was raised"—we have interpreted Christ's resurrection as an erasure of his death. This interpretation of resurrection reminds me of a recently popular song: "Unbreak my heart . . . uncry these tears." Nice sentiment, but hardly realistic. Once something has been broken, it cannot be unbroken; repaired, maybe, but not unbroken. Once tears have been shed, they cannot be unshed; dried, yes; joy renewed, yes; but not uncried. Yet many implicitly interpret the resurrection as an "undying" of the death.

The central confessions of Paul and the other early believers in Jesus, that God had raised Jesus from the dead and that God had made Jesus Lord, were not such sentimental lyrics. They were statements of deep life commitment. We will need to return to the Jewish and Greco-Roman worlds of the first century to understand the language of these confessions and how they could express deep human commitment and hope.

RESURRECTION AND EXALTATION

Separating a discussion of the death of Christ from a discussion of the resurrection will, I hope, allow us to take the real physical death of Jesus more seriously. We will return to the implications of the trauma of that death shortly. For now, it is sufficient to recognize that, for these early believers, the death of the man Jesus of Nazareth was real.[2] The resurrection was not an undying of the death. It was not, that is, a resuscitation of Jesus' physical body. Here is what Paul had to say about the nature of resurrection:

So it is with the resurrection of the dead. What is sown is perishable, what is raised is imperishable. It is sown in dishonor, it is raised in glory. It is sown in weakness, it is raised in power. It is sown a physical body, it is raised a spiritual body. (1 Cor 15:42–44)

What odd language! For, to us, the very word *body* means "physical body." We think of a spirit or a soul living "in" a (physical) body. To speak of a "spiritual body" is, in our ears, something of an oxymoron. It is of crucial importance for us to maintain something of the oxymoronic nature of Paul's language. For when a first-century Jew spoke of resurrection, he or she was not simply speaking of the resuscitation of a physical body (he was dead, but now he's alive; he undied the death). No, the Jewish hope of resurrection was a hope in the apocalyptic intervention of God to bring shalom to the universe. The word *resurrection* invoked a whole constellation of apocalyptic expectation.

Resurrection: A Past and Future Event

Remember the diagram of apocalyptic eschatology from chapter 1? A whole vocabulary developed to depict this apocalyptic eschatology. See illustration 14, which includes some of the language of apocalyptic expectation.

Illustration 14
The Language of Apocalyptic Expectation

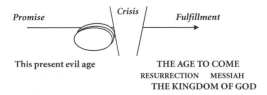

10:1 What Does the Word Mean?

Can you think of other words that have a special meaning in a specific context? For example, here is one word linked with two different words. How does the context alter the meaning of the word?

SUPERMAN.........Lois Lane
SUPERMAN.........Nietzsche

Two very different meanings for the same word! Nietzsche, the philosopher, was hardly talking about a man in blue tights and a cape flying around saving the world and Lois Lane from disaster! Can you think of other examples?

Resurrection was a term that belonged on the right side of the diagram. That is, resurrection was one of the manifestations of the "age to come." It was a sign of the new creation that God would inaugurate when the Messiah came. Thus, when Paul and the early believers proclaimed that "God had raised him from the dead," they were making a claim that God had already inaugurated the messianic age. The age to come had come.[3]

This was a startling claim indeed. The resurrection of Jesus, the Christ, was not, then, a singular resurrection. His resurrection was the "first fruits" of the future resurrection of all God's people. As Paul says to the Corinthians,

> But in fact Christ has been raised from the dead, the first fruits of those who have fallen asleep. . . . For as in Adam all die, so also in Christ shall all be made alive. But each in his own order: Christ the first fruits, then at his coming those who belong to Christ. (1 Cor 15:20–23)

Christ's resurrection was a past event that would be completed in the future when all "those who belong to Christ" would also be raised. A diagram of Paul's expectation might look something like this:

Illustration 15
A Diagram of Paul's Expectation

The Cross of Christ is the moment of apocalyptic crisis that declares the destruction of the rule of sin and death. The Age to Come has already been initiated but is not yet consummated.

Living the Future Now

Pauline scholars have described Paul's sense of time with the phrase "already but not yet." Because Christ has been raised, believers already experience something of the age to come, but this experience is not yet a fully consummated experience. It is somewhat like saying, "We live now because of how we will live because something happened." Such confusions of tenses—past, present, future—can baffle our ordinary sense of time. Perhaps a story will help.

It's holiday time. You've come to visit your mom and just stepped into her home. And immediately you smell it: the Dinner. It's the essence of the family holiday. And the aroma of roasting turkey fills the house. Almost immediately upon your smelling it, your mouth begins to water. You can almost taste that turkey. The promise of the coming dinner orders your day. You don't run down to the corner store for a sneak of ice cream or chocolate candy snack. Even your glands respond involuntarily to the smell of that turkey in the oven.

The proclamation that Christ is the first fruits of the age to come is like saying, "The turkey's in the oven." We can already smell it. Our mouths are already watering. For we are in our mother's home; it is the holiday; and the turkey's in the oven. We may, as dinner gets closer, sneak into the kitchen and steal a bite of the turkey. Not unlike what the early believers in Christ did as they gathered to worship—they got together and said (and sang), "Mmm! Smell that turkey! Doesn't that smell go-o-oood!"

Now you might argue that this is just wishful thinking, that claiming to "smell the turkey" is really no better than hearing, "The check's in the mail." But no, for who among us would walk into our mother's house on a family holiday and be told right at dinnertime, "Sorry, son/daughter, you can't have any turkey today"? These early believers proclaimed that it is God who has put the turkey in the oven; God has promised. Apocalyptic eschatology above all else insists that it is God who will have the last word. God has raised Jesus from the dead. Paul's proclamation is not, "God has promised us a turkey" (we called last weekend and Mom said, "If you come down for Thanksgiving, I'll put the turkey in the oven"), but, "The turkey is already in the oven!"

So the crazy statement "We live now (present) because of how we will live (future) because it did happen (past)" can be reformulated into this: "We organize our holiday morning (present) because of how we will eat at the holiday dinner (future) because mom has already put the turkey in the oven (past)."

Thus, Christ's resurrection (past; mom puts the dinner in the oven) points to the resurrection of all the saints (future; we will eat holiday dinner). But note that these affirmations about the past and the future are not idle statements about what has happened and what will happen. The past and the future both impinge upon the now. Our present is determined by our past and our future. All tenses are determined by God's act in Christ.

10:2 Living Out of the Future

Our expectations for the future often determine our actions in the present. For example, how might the following expectations determine your present actions?

1. The ozone layer of the earth will be gone in ten years.
2. Jobs will be plentiful when you graduate.
3. Jobs will be scarce when you graduate.
4. You will live to be eighty-five years old.
5. You will live to be thirty years old.
6. You will win the lottery next year.
7. The stock market will crash next year.

Illustration 16
Revisiting the Cross Diagram

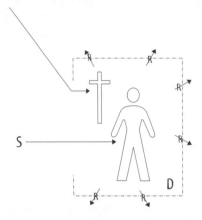

In Paul's understanding of the meaning of Christ's death, we are sinners (S) who have already entered death (D). Christ (†) joins us in our death and dies with us and, when God exalted or raised Christ, the confines of our own death are broken and we are thus "free from death" (R).

Exaltation: Lord of the Universe

It is likely that some of the Gentiles in the churches Paul worked with would have found this apocalyptic vocabulary and imagery as foreign as we find it. Perhaps they, too, would have imagined that a resurrection was nothing more than the miraculous resuscitation of a corpse, an undying of a death—rather than understanding that the word *resurrection* invoked a conviction that God had begun to bring about the new creation promised by prophets of old. It is not surprising, then, that these Gentile believers articulated their confession in somewhat different language. In Paul's Letter to the Philippians he quotes a short hymn that probably reflects the language of these Gentile believers in Christ. In the first stanza of the hymn, Christ descends and lives and dies as an enslaved human (see Phil 2:6–8). But in this hymn, the "death on a cross" (Phil 2:8) is not followed by a resurrection. Rather, these believ-

ers declared that this occurred after Christ's death:

> Therefore God has highly exalted him and has given him the name that is above every name, so that at the name of Jesus every knee should bend, in heaven and on earth and under the earth, and every tongue should confess that Jesus Christ is Lord—to the glory of God the Father. (Phil 2:9–11)

These early believers were convinced that after Jesus was crucified, something dramatic and world changing had happened. Sometimes they described this dramatic something as resurrection; at other times they could describe it as exaltation. These two terms, *resurrection* and *exaltation*, are, then, somewhat synonymous; both refer to a dramatic and world changing action of God in response to the death of this man Jesus.

Each of these terms, however, illumines a particular aspect of the confession of the early believers and of Paul. *Resurrection* describes the results of God's action in apocalyptic language that confounds our sense of time, incorporating past, present, and future into one indivisible reality. *Exaltation* describes the results of God's actions in political language that confounds our sense of space by incorporating the heavenly sphere and the earthly sphere into one coherent reality. Thus, Paul exhorts the Philippians to "conduct yourself as citizens" (Phil 1:27, author's trans.) in a manner that is consistent with the revelation of God in Christ. It is not until later in this letter that we read that although the conduct of the Philippians is clearly conduct in this world, their "citizenship is in heaven" (Phil 3:20).

We could, of course, interpret this spatial confusion simply as some sort of "resident alien" status for the Philippians. That is, although you currently reside on the earth, your true citizenship is elsewhere. Although you currently reside in Japan, your citizenship is in America, so "act like an American." But the culmination of the hymn of Christ's exaltation—"Jesus Christ is Lord"—implies a much more radical meaning.

"Jesus Christ is Lord!" This phrase was the hallmark declaration of the early Christians and constitutes one of the most basic claims of Paul's entire system of thought. When set within the Greco-Roman world, the political and social implications of this exclamation are startling. In the political world of Paul's day, all people knew that Caesar was lord. In the social world of Paul's churches—where much of the membership was made up of slaves—many of the believers had masters (lords) to whom they owed daily obedience. Thus, when such slaves in a world ruled by Rome proclaimed, "Jesus Christ is Lord!" they challenged the most basic realities of their social existence. In the name of a heavenly ruler, they defied their earthly rulers. Bolder even than the Cynic philosopher who defied local political definition by claiming to be a "citizen of the universe," these early believers in Christ declared a new social and political order that rendered all present lordships impotent: "At the name of Jesus every knee should bend, in heaven and on earth and under the earth, and every tongue should confess that Jesus Christ is Lord, to the glory of God the Father" (Phil 2:10–11).

10:3 Social Revolution

Describe how the confession "Jesus is Lord!" might sound in Caesar's ears. In a slave owner's ears. Why is this a radical confession?

The language and imagery of resurrection and exaltation both point to the ultimate sovereignty of the God of Israel over all earthly rule and authority, just as certainly as over the apocalyptic powers of sin and death. See how Paul combines these political and apocalyptic images in his Letter to the Corinthians:

> But in fact Christ has been raised from the dead, the first fruits of those who have fallen asleep. . . . For as in Adam all die, so also in Christ shall all be made alive. But each in his own order: Christ the first fruits, then at his coming those who belong to Christ. Then comes the end, when he delivers the kingdom to God the Father after destroying every rule and every authority and power. For he must reign until he has put all his enemies under his feet. The last enemy to be destroyed is death. . . . When all things are subjected to him, then the Son himself will also be subjected to him who put all things under him, that God may be everything to every one.
>
> "Death is swallowed up in victory."
> "O death, where is thy victory?
> O death, where is thy sting?"
>
> The sting of death is sin, and the power of sin is the law. But thanks be to God, who gives us the victory through our Lord Jesus Christ. (1 Cor 15:20–28, 54b–57)

The central confessions of Paul and other early believers in Christ were potent declarations that, in Christ, God had inaugurated a new reality. In order to express their understanding of this new reality, the early believers drew on the apocalyptic language of Judaism (resurrection) and the political language of Greco-Roman society (exaltation and lordship). The affirmation that "God has raised him from the dead" declared that although this new reality would be fully realized in the future, it was already in effect in the present. The affirmation that "God has exalted him and made him Lord" declared that although this new reality was "in heaven," it also determined life here on earth.

This dual-toned confession—that Christ was raised and that Christ has been exalted—addresses the original definition of righteousness. God's goal is to bring shalom to the entire cosmos. God has created the universe and intends to weave the whole of reality into an unbroken fabric of peace. But in Paul's view, the apocalyptic powers of sin and death had wrested the universe away from God's control. Sin and death have thwarted God's dream of shalom. God's raising of Christ from death has defeated the power of death. Christ has been exalted over the powers of sin and death, and the universe has now been restored to the Creator who made it. In Christ, God has redeemed the world.[4]

"FOR EVERYONE WHO HAS FAITH"

The confession of the resurrection ("already but not yet") and/or the exaltation ("in heaven but also on earth") of Christ was the defining moment for the early believers. As Paul writes to the Romans,

> If you confess with your lips that Jesus is Lord and believe in your heart that God raised him from the dead, you will be saved. (Rom 10:9)

From our perspective, this perhaps looks like an extraordinarily easy way to be saved. Certainly, when compared with a rigorous obedience to the law, a verbal confession and intellectual assent seem ridiculously simple. Remember the dancer? What if she were told, "Silly girl, you don't need to practice dancing all the time! All you need to do is just believe in your heart that you will be a professional dancer, and voilà! you're a professional dancer"?

Such a simple-minded view is not at all what Paul or the early believers in Jesus meant by confessing or believing in Christ, but it is too often the way people today have understood the meaning of the word *faith*. One of the reasons it is necessary to articulate the meaning of resurrection and exaltation with such care is that in the centuries since Paul wrote, the meaning of these two terms has (at least in popular understanding) become severely watered down. To believe in the resurrection has meant simply to give some kind of cognitive assent that Jesus' corpse came back to life: He walked out of the tomb. To confess Jesus' lordship has frequently meant that "I have exalted him in my heart; Jesus is number one in my life." But the terms *resurrection* and *exaltation* cannot be so easily psychologized. For Paul and other early believers, these terms pointed to a world-changing event—not just to a private religious experience. They express hope in a radically new social order—not just a privately held personal opinion. Thus, in order to understand these confessions, which sit at the center of Paul's thought, we will need to understand what Paul means when he uses *believe* and *faith*.

A Perceptive Faith

Try asking someone you know to define *faith* or *belief*. What does it mean, for instance, to "believe in" God? What does it mean to "have faith"? More often than not, when this question is asked, the response will be something like, "Well, to have faith in something means to believe in it even though there is no real proof that it's true. You just have to believe." As with most half-truths, this understanding of faith does express some truth. Paul himself says, "We look not to the things that are seen but to the things that are unseen" (2 Cor 4:18). But often this observation that faith has something to do with committing oneself to unseen things is interpreted as meaning that one is to have blind faith. That is, true faith, in this misunderstanding, is a faith that believes in spite of what one knows to be true otherwise. So some will believe in a seven-day creation of the world some four thousand years ago—in spite of the fact that all scientific evidence indicates that the origins of our universe are much more ancient and much more complicated than a seven-day creation would allow. True faith, according to this view, means that I, as an intelligent person, choose to blind myself to all scientific evidence to the contrary and that I simply believe something because "the Bible says so."

Given what we've already learned about Paul and his commitment to the accurate perception of things, however, you should already have some sense that Paul would be very much opposed to a faith that is born out of blindness or of a refusal to acknowledge things as they really are. In fact, Paul's understanding of faith is directly related to his conviction that under the power of sin humans misperceive both God and the world. To believe blindly is to misperceive. To be under the power of sin is to exercise a "bad faith"—a faith that is misplaced precisely because it is blind.[5]

The revelation of God in Jesus Christ was a revelation of the way things really are. To witness this revelation is to recognize and acknowledge that God justifies the ungodly apart from the law; it is to see clearly for the first time that God is a God of grace, that humans are creatures of this God, and that God has created these limited human creatures for good. Paul's notion of faith is directly related to this revelation. The revelation is a moment of great Aha! This is the moment of grace, when we recognize the radical freedom of God in accepting and calling the ungodly. Faith describes the commitment one makes to live in light of this moment of grace. Faith is a commitment to refuse to continue to live in the blindness of sin and to live instead out of the clear perception of God's grace.

Near the beginning of chapter 5, the notion of sin as a disease was compared to the situation of an alcoholic or other addict. If I am mired in an addiction, then I am unable to acknowledge the truth about my addiction. I live in a blind faith that "I can kick this habit any time I want to." And no matter how much evidence to the contrary someone tries to give me, I still insist on living in my own blindness. The first real moment of possibility comes when I finally can stand and say, as in an AA meeting, "My name is _____ , and I am an alcoholic." Once I can admit the truth about myself, I have taken the first step toward recovery. The recovery is not complete at this point, however. I must go away from the meeting and back into my life—my family, my job, my friends, my school—and live responsibly, with the knowledge that I am an alcoholic and that if I continue to drink, I will destroy my life. This is where true faith comes in. To make the

10:4 The Commitment of Faith

Can you remember a moment of revelation in your life? (If not, ask someone older than you to tell you about one of their revelatory moments.) Did this moment of revelation change your life in noticeable ways? If so, how? Do you still live out of your experience of that revelation? If you do, then you are living the life of faith in relation to that moment of grace.

confession "I am an alcoholic" is a moment of revelation. To live in light of this confession is to live the life of faith. Faith is an active response to the revelation of grace.

We can also state this in terms of what we learned about God being a God without a measuring stick. To experience the revelation of Christ is to come to the realization that God does not measure and that a life lived according to the flesh (i.e., according to human measurements) is a false life. For instance, what would life look like if I believed—that is, lived in light of the fact—that

> grades do not determine my worth;
>
> the size of my paycheck does not determine my worth;
>
> my relationships do not determine my worth?

What would life look like if we believed about each other—that is, lived in light of the fact—that

> your physical appearance does not determine your value;
>
> the size of your house or where you live does not tell me who you are;
>
> your gender or your ethnicity or your sexual orientation or your political views do not define you?

What would human social life look like if we trusted the revelation of God that Paul claims has occurred in Christ?

But herein lies a crucial difficulty in Paul's notion of faith. To have faith is to commit oneself to a view of human reality that goes against much of what our society tells us is important. To believe in God's revelation of righteousness means that we dare to challenge our society's definition of what makes for a good human life. Thus, faith does not necessarily

lead to a life of inner peace and harmony. Indeed, as Paul frequently indicates, the life of faith in God's grace often leads the believer into deadly conflict with a society that is still blinded by the power of sin.

A Suffering Faith

If it is a popular misconception that to believe is to exercise blind faith, then a popular misconception of the consequences of faith is that a true faith is one that will lead to a sweet and happy life for the believer. Not so, says Paul. Indeed, the life of faith often leads one into suffering. Listen to what Paul has to say about the life of faith:

> But we have this treasure in earthen vessels, to show that the transcendent power belongs to God and not to us. We are afflicted in every way, but not crushed; perplexed, but not driven to despair; persecuted, but not forsaken; struck down, but not destroyed; always carrying in the body the death of Jesus, so that the life of Jesus may also be manifested in our bodies. For while we live we are always being given up to death for Jesus' sake, so that the life of Jesus may be manifested in our mortal flesh. (2 Cor 4:7–11)

In short, the life of faith, in Paul's view, often leads one into suffering and persecution. Why, then, would anyone want to live the life of faith? Why trust in a way of life that entails suffering?

Again, the illustration of the addict or alcoholic might be of help to us here. Once the addict acknowledges his addiction, life begins to change. And the changes are difficult changes that require immense commitment. The most obvious change, of course, is that the addict has to retrain his own behavior. But other changes are necessary as well—and some of these changes involve the people around the addict. Whether it is giving up alcohol or cigarettes or drugs or whatever one might be addicted to, the addiction has occurred in a social context of some sort. And as is frequently the case, the addict's friends and family have come to expect the addict to act in addicted ways. This social context is part of the overall addiction. Now, this does not mean that in order to break an addiction, we must completely escape our social context. But it does mean that our individual choice to break an addiction also affects the people with whom we interact. Either they support us in our efforts to break the addiction or they (either directly or subtly) resist our newfound life.

In Paul's understanding of human life, when we acknowledge that, in Christ, God revealed the truth about humanity, we simultaneously acknowledge that our society has taught us (and we have wholeheartedly adopted) a seriously flawed understanding of what it means to be human. To say yes to God's revelation in Christ (= faith) is to say no to our society's understanding of life. And this confession has at least two consequences for our lives. First, our yes sets us against our former understanding of life. This means that we must continually recognize the deadliness of that former understanding and retrain our eyes to focus on the new perception of life that has been revealed

in Christ. We continue, that is, to confront and acknowledge the death of Christ: the deadliness of the misperception caused by sin.

But there is another, related consequence of our yes as well. To the extent that we make public our new understanding of life, others in our society may interpret us as troublemakers. Just as a newly recovering addict must make a stand among his friends or family members who were part of the addiction (those with whom he smoke, drank, or did drugs), so the one who says yes to God's revelation in Christ cannot escape saying no among those who continue to define human life according to human measurements.

In Paul's understanding, Christ's crucifixion was no accident; it was the result of a cosmic conflict between God and those mighty forces of sin and death. It was a cosmic conflict that took place here on this historical plane among human actors. Thus, when Paul says that he has "been crucified with Christ," he implicitly acknowledges that he, too, has entered into this cosmic conflict. He has seen the lie of sin and death and has cast his lot in with the God who is a God without a measuring stick, the God who is (and has always been) a God of grace. This ongoing conflict is a part of the reality of this

---

10:5 Are You A Troublemaker?

Read this brief story about a king of Israel who called a prophet of God a troublemaker:

When Ahab saw Elijah, Ahab said to him, "Is it you, you troubler of Israel?" He answered, "I have not troubled Israel; but you have, and your father's house, because you have forsaken the commandments of the LORD." (I Kgs 18:17–18)

History is filled with the stories of men and women who, because they were committed faithfully to a vision, have caused trouble for the powers of the world. Martin Luther King Jr. is one example of such a faithful troublemaker. Can you think of other examples? Explain how faith can lead someone to be a troublemaker. Why does such faith lead to suffering?

"already but not yet" perception of time. The complete victory over death is still in the future. The outcome of the conflict between God and death is already determined; but the conflict is ongoing, it has not yet run its full course.

Living under the blindness of sin, we assumed that we were living in the real world—the only world that existed. There was no conflict for us, because our society sustained our (mis)perception. As with the sign that reads, "The bird in the the the bush" (illustration 13), we were convinced that our first readings were correct. But once we see the light and acknowledge that sin has blinded us, we can no longer accept the "obviousness" of that former reading. We now know the truth and live in light of that revelation. And this means that we are—whether we want to be or not—in direct conflict with those for whom that former world is still the real world. We may now recognize that neither ourselves nor others are defined by human measurements . . . but the registrar and graduate schools, the bank and credit agencies, our neighbors and our families still measure human worth in these terms.

Thus, our yes to the revelation of this God of grace results in a perception of ourselves and of others that confounds others in our society. It may, as it certainly did in Paul's life, result in real suffering. The question is, Would we rather live in light of the truth—even if it means suffering? Or is ignorance really bliss? From Paul's perspective, ignorance (especially the ignorance of blind faith) is never bliss. His understanding of the fulfillment of human life was, in some significant ways, in conflict with the Greco-Roman philosophers who saw security, serenity, and inner peace as the primary goal of human life. For Paul, the epitome of human life does not lie in personal serenity. No, according to Paul's Jewish tradition, human life only finds fulfillment in partnership with

this God in God's righteous determination to bring shalom to the whole universe. The ultimate goal of all human life is to share in the glory of God as it will eventually be expressed in the entire cosmos. This, then, is the hope of the life of faith: that God's righteousness might be realized in all of the cosmos.

"HOPE DOES NOT DISAPPOINT"

In Rom 5:1–5 Paul briefly summarizes his understanding of righteousness, faith, and hope.

> Therefore since we are justified by faith, we have peace with God through our Lord Jesus Christ. Through him we have obtained access to this grace in which we stand, and we rejoice in our hope of sharing the glory of God. More than that, we rejoice in our sufferings, knowing that suffering produces endurance, and endurance produces character, and character produces hope, and hope does not disappoint us, because God's love has been poured into our hearts through the Holy Spirit which has been given to us.

What is this hope that Paul says "does not disappoint us"? Well, do you remember the turkey in the oven? The hope is that we will sit down with our family and enjoy the holiday dinner. But the hope is more than this.

This volume has used numerous illustrations about how we function in the world as individuals in relationship with other humans. These illustrations have, I hope, helped you to understand some of the logical dynamics in Paul's thought. But there is one significant drawback to using such illustrations. Paul is interested in the lives of individual humans. But his thought is not primarily focused on helping individual humans to fulfill their individual potential. In this regard, Paul's thought is somewhat at odds with our present therapeutic culture. When you go see a therapist, the therapist's primary concern is to help you function better as an individual and perhaps even to assist you in finding some peace and happiness. The hope you seek in a therapist's office is a hope for better relationships or happier life. Now, Paul would certainly not be opposed to such things. But the hope of Paul is the hope not for his own happiness and peace but, rather, for the "glory of God." The glory of God is not unrelated to God's creation, of course. Indeed, the renewing of all creation is a constituent part of God's glory that is yet to be revealed in all of the universe. See what Paul says about the hope of human freedom, the renewal of creation, and God's glory in Rom 8:18–25:

> I consider the sufferings of this present time are not worth comparing with the glory that is to be revealed to us. For the creation waits with eager longing for the revealing of the children of God; . . . because the creation itself will be set free from its bondage and decay and obtain the glorious liberty of the children of God. We know that the whole creation has been groaning in travail together until now; and not only the creation, but we ourselves, who have the first fruits of the Spirit, groan inwardly as we wait for adoption and the redemption of our bodies. For in this hope we are saved.

The hope of human freedom is directly related to the liberation of creation from its own bondage and decay. And it is this restoration of all creation—human and nonhuman—that will redound to the glory of God.

Such an understanding of salvation is quite distinct from the individual salvation that is so frequently proclaimed today. For Paul the goal is not "me, myself, and mine"—eternal life for me; freedom for myself; and a salvation that is mine. No, Israel had always anticipated a corporate salvation. And Paul, in good Jewish fashion, anticipates God's shalom for the whole of creation.

I still remember when I first grasped this idea. One day, when my children were preschoolers, I was driving somewhere, and both of my daughters were riding in the back seat of the car. Earlier that winter I had broken one of those giant toothbrushes that we use to clear ice and snow off a car. You know the kind, a scraper on one end of a long stick and a brush running along the edge of the other end. Not being a particularly neat person, and being somewhat aggravated that my favorite giant toothbrush had snapped in two, I had simply tossed the two broken pieces into the back seat. Now my daughters had each grabbed one of the pieces and were proceeding to bang on the windows, the back of the front seat, and no doubt on each other's heads as well. Eventually one of them exclaimed in anguish, "Mine's broken!" Whereupon the other one, investigating her own piece quickly, screamed in even greater anguish, "Mine's broken too!" And I, being a better theologian than I am a mother (for what kind of mother would let her preschoolers bang around in the car with broken sticks!), laughed and explained, "No, you don't each have a broken thing. There's just one broken toothbrush, and you each have a piece of it." As you might imagine, this little explanation did absolutely no good at calming my two preschoolers. But it did teach me a lesson.

Too frequently we have understood sin or disease or brokenness as an individual thing—as though everyone had their own little broken toothbrush. But the truth of the matter, according to Paul, is that there is only one giant toothbrush. And all the brokenness in the world—human brokenness and ecological disaster—is broken off the same thing. God's glory will be fully revealed when—and only when—the whole thing is put back together again, when there is not one piece missing. God's glory will be revealed in perfect shalom.

This means that the hope that does not disappoint is a hope for the entire cosmos. No one who has understood God's love and grace could be satisfied with some merely personal salvation of his or her individual self. No, the revelation of God in Christ is a revelation of God's ultimate renewal of the entire cosmos. Faith is the confidence that, in Christ, God has revealed the truth about God and about humanity. Faith means living in the now, based on that Aha! moment of grace in the past. Hope is the extension of this confidence into the future—not only for ourselves but for the whole of creation.

CONCLUSION

Paul's proclamation of Christ was founded upon his own experience of a revelatory moment when he gained a radically new perception of himself, of the God that he worshiped, and of the whole of creation. In his efforts to communicate the meaning of this experience, Paul drew on the vocabulary of his Jewish heritage and expectations as well as on the language of early Christian worship. In Christ's death on the cross, Paul perceived the death of all humanly determined measurements. God and God's grace is (and always has been) limitless. Once humans perceive their Creator accurately, they are able to relate to one another in new ways, ways that are not determined by attempts to measure up to some external standards. As Paul wrote to the Galatians, neither Jew nor Greek, neither slave nor free, neither male nor female (Gal 3:28). All humans—both Jew and Gentile—are to be included in God's covenant community and are called to participate with God in bringing shalom to this world. In Christ's resurrection and exaltation, Paul perceived the victory of God over all foes and the ultimate shalom of all creation.

The human responses to this revelation of God in Christ are the responses of faith and hope. The individual moment of grace—no matter how overwhelming at the moment—is not, in itself, enough. In order for grace to take root in human life, in human society, individual humans must say yes to the moment of grace. The human response of faith acknowledges that the moment of grace is more than a "neat experience"—it is the determinative revelation about the whole of human life. To believe that God has raised Christ from the dead is to commit oneself to live out of that gracious reality—not only in relation to God but in relation to oneself and to one's neighbors. To confess that "Jesus Christ is Lord!" is to declare the confident hope that the vision of life revealed in Jesus Christ is the consummation of all creation. The victory over the forces of sin and death, though not yet fully manifest, has already been won. And though present human experience may still be riddled with suffering and humiliation, hope in the reality that God has revealed in Christ leads Paul to declare that through it all God's loving grace will triumph.

> For I am sure that neither death, nor life, nor angels, nor principalities, nor things present, nor things to come, nor powers, nor height, nor depth, nor anything else in all creation, will be able to separate us from the love of God in Christ Jesus our Lord. (Rom 8:38–39)

The love of God in Christ Jesus our Lord: This is the consequence of God's act in Christ. That humans may live and know the reality of love. And as we come to the end of this study of what Paul thought about God and about human life, we must turn to the topic of love. For Paul says that "faith, hope, love abide, these three; but the greatest of these is love" (1 Cor 13:13).

READING CHECK:

☑ Why is resurrection not the same as resuscitation? What is the meaning of resurrection in Paul's apocalyptic vocabulary?

☑ Why is the confession that "Jesus Christ is Lord!" a radical social statement?

☑ What does it mean to believe in Christ? How is faith related to grace?

☑ Why does faith sometimes lead to suffering?

☑ How is hope related to shalom?

part three

Summary and Review

SUMMARY

No thinker can be explained solely in terms of his or her background and training. If one simply reiterates what one has learned, then there can be no creative contribution to intellectual thought. From beginning to end, Paul was a Jew. His fundamental beliefs and dreams were rooted in Judaism. But Paul also interacted with other cultures as well. He may not have exchanged ideas directly with any Greco-Roman philosopher. But he was engaged in the same conversation about what it means to be human in a world that is diverse, often inhumane, and confusing. Paul's creative contribution emerged in this dialogue between his Jewish heritage and the Greco-Roman context.

Paul tells us very little about his life before his encounter with Christ. Surely he had already begun to reflect on the relationships between Jews and Gentiles, between the Jewish law and Gentile ethics. Unfortunately, we do not know exactly what he thought before God revealed Christ to Paul. Whether this revelation crystallized what Paul had already begun to think about, or whether the revelation was a radically disruptive moment in Paul's thinking, we simply cannot know. We do know, however, that in Paul's letters to his churches he articulated a particularly powerful and creative approach to the problems of human life.

Humans experience despair. The cause of this despair is sin: We misperceive the God who has created us, and thus misperceive ourselves and each other. Whether a person is a member of the Jewish community or not, she or he is nevertheless infected with this misperception. It is inescapable. Worse, it appears to be irremediable. For the One who could rescue us is the very One whom we misperceive. But this gracious God has sent a mediator who can overcome our misperception and reveal to us the truth about God's grace. This one sent from God, the one who is called Christ, has entered fully into the human situation of impotence, death, and despair. He has joined with us at our most vulnerable point. And in doing so, he has become the means by which God has revealed grace to us: We experience God's righteousness apart from the law. Our misperception is shattered, and we are free now to commit ourselves in faith to live together as God intended. We look forward in the hope of shalom for the universe.

Thus does the revelation of God in Christ bring us full circle back to the righteousness of this shalom-making God. Human despair is turned to hope, death is turned to life, and defeat is turned to victory. Victory does not come through mastery of the self or of the passions, as the philosophers contended. Rather, victory comes through Christ: the revelation of God's righteous grace in bringing shalom to the whole cosmos.

REVIEW

A. Terms and Concepts

1. gospel
2. conversion
3. mystical experience
4. call
5. apostle
6. Pharisee
7. Christ (as a term)
8. grace
9. *charismata*
10. resurrection
11. exaltation
12. age to come
13. redemption
14. justification apart from the law

15. the scandal of grace
16. co-crucifixion
17. cross
18. Abraham
19. reconciliation
20. baptism
21. living according to the flesh
22. living according to the Spirit
23. faith
24. hope
25. Jesus is Lord

B. Making Connections

1. Watch the movie *Tender Mercies.* Drawing from the plot of the movie for your answers, identify the scenes, relationships, and events that best illustrate the following concepts in Paul's thought: sin, law, death, resurrection, righteousness, grace, faith, hope.

2. Watch the movie *Places in the Heart.* How do the weaknesses of the various characters in the movie become their strengths, their *charismata*? What role(s) does the community play in this movie? How is resurrection imagined in the movie—and what does it mean for future community life?

3. Read the novel *The French Lieutenant's Woman,* by John Fowles. Describe the scene toward the end of the book when Charles Smithson is in the chapel, and relate it to Paul's understanding of the cross.

4. Look back at the essay you wrote for the part 1 review on dream-desire-discipline, and at the reflections you wrote for the part 2 review on how your dream could be (or has been) thwarted. Now, imagine how Paul's notion of Christ might reveal a "grace apart from the law" in relation to this dream. Write a short story that expresses this hope.

Moving Ahead

"Love Increasing in Knowledge"

Righteousness—grace—faith—hope—shalom. These terms describe the vision that one man had for human life. His vision has been a particularly potent one for Western civilization. Throughout the past two millennia, thinkers have turned to his intellectual and religious vision—either to reinterpret it for a new day or to attack it for its insufficiencies. What, then, are we today to make of the Apostle Paul and his vision? In what ways might his vision be of meaning today? Although there could well be several answers to these questions, I want, in these last pages, to suggest two important insights that we might observe in the thought of Paul.

Thinking Clearly

Central to Paul's thought is his insistence that both the damning and the salvation of humanity are integrally related to how humans think. The evils and ills of humankind are not the result, in Paul's view, of a failure of human will. Nor is the good in human existence simply the result of good training. Paul describes humane society as life according to the Spirit and inhumane society as life according to the flesh. Although we might use different language to describe these opposing options for human society, although we might want to allow more gray areas to be interposed between these two extreme options, at some point we all rely upon some foundational understanding of what is good and what is evil.

An engagement with Paul's thought demands that we do some of our own thinking about what makes for a humane society. And this means that we must also wrestle with the question of why society is, all too often, inhumane. What we learn from Paul is this: Not only is it crucial for us to think about such matters; the very act of thinking, and thinking clearly, is crucial to the functioning of a humane society. In short, if we think perversely, we will live perversely. We can see the progression in what Paul writes to the Romans:

> For those who live according to the flesh set their minds on the things of the flesh, but those who live according to the Spirit set their minds on the things of the Spirit. (Rom 8:5)

To live well, we must think well. This is one of the central insights of Paul's thought. Human ills are not just the result of emotions gone out of control, or of bad manners, or of innate evil, or even of a willed desire to do evil. Nor is human good the result of well-trained emotions or manners ("Just be nice") or of an inflexible obedience to a superego. The determining factor in human life is the question "On what is your mind set?" or "How do you think?"

> To set the mind on the flesh is death, but to set the mind on the Spirit is life and peace. (Rom 8:6)

According to Paul, our society silently conspires to train us to set our mind on the "flesh," that is, to measure ourselves against other humans (and measure other humans against ourselves). Herein lies our "death." But God, Paul says, has made plain to us that God, as our Creator, is the one who determines our existence, our identity, and our worth. To set our mind on the Spirit is to accept our status as creatures of this Creator. Herein, according to Paul, lies the key to life and peace.

Paul's apocalyptic vision of the power of sin and death and of the victory of God over these powers may seem foreign and fantastic to us. But whether we accept Paul's particular mythology or not, we can still learn from the way he goes about thinking of human life. In short, how we think about the beginning and the end of human existence is cru-

cial to how we live in this world. The questions of the origin and the end of the world are more than either scientific curiosities or issues of idle personal opinion. These questions determine how we live with one another in the world.

What do your theories about the beginning of the world say about human life? What are the ethical consequences of your views of earth's origins? What do you believe about the nature of human death? And what difference does that belief make in how you treat your neighbor, in how you treat yourself? Does death make all of life a competition (to make sure you win in the end)? Does your view of death, either your own or that of others, enable you to live more fully and more humanely? Whatever else we learn from this study of the Apostle Paul, we can learn this: How we think about life and death determines how we live and how we die.

The question of how and what we think, then, is not an idle question that we reflect upon in some ivory tower, removed from the real stuff of human life. It is not something that we do in school—though schoolwork should aid us in our ability to think well. Learning to think, and to think well, about these foundational issues is crucial to humane living. But learning to think, and think well, consists of more than merely garnering masses of knowledge or wearing vestments of wisdom. The center and goal of our thinking must lie in what Paul calls love.

An Intelligent Love

In his First Letter to the Corinthians, Paul includes a beautiful hymn to love. It is a poem that you have probably heard before:

> If I speak in the tongues of humans and of angels but have not love, I am a noisy gong or a clanging cymbal. And if I have prophetic powers, and understand all mysteries and all

knowledge, and if I have all faith, so as to re-move mountains, but have not love, I am nothing. If I give away all I have, and if I de-liver my body to be burned, but have not love, I gain nothing.

Love is patient and kind; love is not jealous or boastful; it is not arrogant or rude. Love does not insist on its own way; it is not irrita-ble or resentful; it does not rejoice at wrong, but rejoices in the right. Love bears all things, believes all things, hopes all things, endures all things.

Love never ends; as for prophecy, it will pass away; as for tongues, they will cease; as for knowledge, it will pass away. For our knowl-edge is imperfect and our prophecy is im-perfect; but when the perfect comes, the imperfect will pass away. When I was a child, I spoke like a child, I thought like a child, I reasoned like a child; when I became a man, I gave up childish ways. For now we see in a mirror dimly, but then face to face. Now I know in part; then I shall understand fully, even as I have been fully understood. So faith, hope, love abide, these three; but the greatest of these is love. (1 Corinthians 13)

A beautiful poem, but one that I am hesitant to quote. Not because the poem lacks in ei-ther beauty or intellectual merit but because our culture has so romanticized love. Love has become a sentimental emotion. But Paul's notion of love bears our attention, precisely because it is a love that subverts all mere sentimentality.

Paul's poem on love can teach us many things. It certainly checks any inclination we might have to equate knowledge with power in a simplistic fashion. Lest we think that Paul's insistence that we have "transformed minds" (see Rom 12:1–2) means that our knowledge gives us power over others, Paul reminds us that without love, knowledge is nothing. And lest we think that our present knowledge is sufficient (even the knowledge revealed by God in Christ), Paul reminds us

that our knowledge is imperfect. The goal of thinking well is not the acquiring of knowl-edge. Rather, the goal of thinking well, in-deed the goal of acquiring knowledge, is to learn to love. So Paul prayed for his friends in Philippi,

> And it is my prayer that your love may abound more and more, with all knowledge and discernment. (Phil 1:9)

Knowledge, in Paul's view, leads to love, not to the ability to oppress or manipulate. Love, in Paul's view, requires discernment. Love, like faith, is not blind. Indeed, loving well demands clear vision. Loving well can only emerge from thinking well. Love, then, is not primarily an emotion. It is the human action that flows out of perceiving others according to the Spirit. One scholar has described this kind of "loving thought" as "caring percep-tion." In short, because we perceive our-selves and each other according to the Spirit rather than according to the flesh, we are fi-nally able to love the other (and ourselves) without oppressing or manipulating him or her for our own end. The freedom that comes from trusting the God of grace is a freedom that enables us to perceive others as they are. And to perceive well, in Paul's view, always leads to loving well.

Thoughtful lives; thought-full lives; lives full of thought. Thinking carefully about who we are as humans and what it means to live and die in this world will determine how we live with one another. We cannot train our-selves to be thoughtful apart from learning to think well. For the Apostle Paul, the revelation of God in Jesus Christ transforms our think-ing so that we become constrained by love.

> For the love of Christ controls us, because we are convinced that one has died for all; therefore all have died. And he died for all, that those who live might live no longer for themselves but for him who for their sake died and was raised.

From now on, therefore, we regard no one from a human point of view; even though we once regarded Christ from a human point of view, we regard him thus no longer. Therefore, if any one is in Christ, that one is a new creation; the old has passed away, behold, the new has come. All this is from God, who through Christ reconciled us to himself and gave us the ministry of reconciliation; that is, God was in Christ reconciling the world to himself, not counting their trespasses against them, and entrusting to us the message of reconciliation. So we are ambassadors for Christ, God making his appeal through us. We beseech you on behalf of Christ, be reconciled to God. For our sake he made him to be sin who knew no sin, so that in him we might become the righteousness of God. (2 Cor 5:14–21)

This was Paul's vision, that humans become the righteousness of God, that humans become active participants with God in bringing shalom to the cosmos, that humans be reconciled with their Creator and controlled by love.

What is your vision? What controls you? How will you think about life, death, and the purpose of humanity? What thoughts fill you? What thoughts will lead you to lead thoughtful lives?

Endnotes

INTRODUCTION: GETTING STARTED

1. I will treat the following as genuine Pauline letters: 1 Thessalonians, Galatians, 1 and 2 Corinthians, Philippians, Philemon, and Romans.

2. You may want to supplement this material with other information on the history and culture of the first-century Jewish and Greco-Roman worlds, either through lectures or additional readings or both. See the "Suggested Reading" list at the end of the book.

3. See M. Adler and C. van Doren, *How to Read a Book: The Classic Guide to Intelligent Reading* (rev. ed.; New York: Simon & Schuster, 1967), 96–115, for an excellent discussion of the difference between a term and a word and the importance of coming to terms with an author. I borrow this language from Adler and van Doren.

4. This is, for instance, similar to the necessity of understanding the terms *id, ego,* and *superego* in order to understand Sigmund Freud's thought. What are some other examples of particular terms that you must understand in order to relate to a writer's thought?

5. See the recent book by Marcus Borg, *The God We Never Knew* (San Francisco: HarperSanFrancisco, 1997).

CHAPTER 1: PAUL THE JEW

1. The Pharisees were loosely associated scholars of the Jewish law, particularly concerned with maintaining the oral traditions that sought to guard the sanctity and obedience of this law.

2. *Apostle* means "one who is sent."

3. Jews who lived outside Palestine are referred to as Diaspora Jews.

4. YHWH is the name of God that God gave to Moses. It is known as the Tetragrammaton and is translated LORD in English translations. See Exod 3:14.

5. The Jewish historian Josephus described four philosophies of Judaism in Palestine during this period (*Jewish War* 8). See a good description of the varieties of first-century Judaism in Martin S. Jaffee, *Early Judaism* (Upper Saddle River, N.J.: Prentice-Hall, 1997).

6. The Qumran community would say something quite different.

7. Especially those included in the Septuagint, a Greek translation of the Hebrew Scriptures.

8. The Greek word *christianoi,* from which we get *Christian,* had not yet been used to describe these believers.

CHAPTER 2: RIGHTEOUSNESS

1. In the period recorded in the Hebrew Bible, this people was called Israel; in Paul's day they were more frequently referred to as Jews. Since we are studying Paul, I will use the terms interchangeably.

2. See Rom 3:3 for a similar question by Paul: "Will their [Israel's] faithlessness nullify the faithfulness of God?"

3. See Jeremiah 2–3.

CHAPTER 3: LAW

1. Here "law" refers to the Torah—the law given by God to Moses on Mount Sinai. Paul uses the Greek term *nomos* in a variety of ways, and not always in reference to Torah. My treatment of *law* in Paul assumes that (a) Paul's primary point of reference was the Mosaic law, the Torah, but also that (b) it will help to understand Paul's point of view if we understand how law functions in human society. Thus, I will develop various

modern analogies in order to illumine why Paul and his Jewish contemporaries were grateful for the law.

2. Admittedly, the covenant between students and an institution may lean more toward a contract, for the relational aspect in this covenant is generally less than that in marriage, friendship, or family covenants. Nevertheless, this example provides a helpful analogy to the function of the law.

3. See Num 14:17–19.

4. The notion of individual salvation in Christianity is strong. It will be important, however, to note that Paul's understanding of shalom, though applying to individuals, is fundamentally corporate and cosmic. Christianity has, in many ways, lost this fundamental emphasis of Paul.

CHAPTER 4: PAUL AMONG THE GENTILES

1. The features of Greco-Roman philosophy identified below were shared by all of the major philosophical groups during this period, although each philosophy nuanced these themes in a particular way.

2. It is from this expression that we get *cosmopolitan: cosmo* = world and *politan* = citizen.

3. You might recall one of the questions in chapter 1, where you were asked to consider the differences between how Americans use English and how the British use English. Just because the Americans don't have "lifts" doesn't mean that they don't have things (elevators) that function exactly like England's lifts. Different cultures name things in their own way, even if they use the same formal language.

4. Lucretius, *De rerum natura* 1053–1070. Cited in Martha C. Nussbaum, *The Therapy of Desire: Theory and Practice in Hellenistic*

Ethics (Princeton: Princeton University Press, 1994), 197–98.

5. Trans. R. H. Charles, in *The Apocrypha and Pseudepigrapha of the Old Testament* (ed. R. H. Charles; 2 vols.; Oxford: Clarendon, 1913).

6. It would therefore be anachronistic to attribute the formal Christian doctrine of original sin to Paul or *2 Baruch.*

7. Quoted in Nussbaum, *Therapy of Desire,* 137.

8. Paul was not the only Jew who emphasized the importance of human rationality. Others, such as Philo and the author of the Maccabees, also highlighted the crucial role of the intellect and reason in the life of faith.

9. Epictetus, *Discourses* 3.20.12, 15–17 (Oldfather, Loeb Classical Library, emphasis added).

10. See Nussbaum, *Therapy of Desire.*

11. Epictetus, *Enchiridion* 1.5, emphasis added.

CHAPTER 5: SIN

1. See illustration 6.

2. The primary difference is that Judaism understands forgiveness to come directly from God and in relation to the covenant of the Torah and the rituals associated with the Torah, whereas Christians see Jesus as the necessary mediator of forgiveness. Another difference is that Judaism understands the relationship with God in the context of a relationship to the people Israel. In Western Christianity, the relationship is more frequently understood to be a private, personal relationship between the individual and God (or Jesus).

3. The guilt I experience is an objective guilt under the law. Whether or not I feel guilty (i.e., subjective guilt) is another matter. The fact that ancient Mediterranean society was, according to sociologists, an honor-shame culture rather than a guilt culture does not destroy the dynamic of objective guilt in relation to law.

4. The narration of this situation of spousal abuse is a simplistic one for the purposes of illustration. Certainly not every husband who abuses his wife feels sorrow. But if we are to listen to the story of some abusers, then we discover that they have felt sorrow. Also, it is important to recognize that although in the majority of spousal-abuse situations the husband abuses the wife, the reverse also happens.

5. And unfortunately, the woman may also reenter another abusive relationship. Forgiveness doesn't help; but leaving does not, by itself, solve her problems.

6. Refer to the earlier brief discussion about eschatology and the differences between prophetic eschatology and apocalyptic eschatology in chapter 1.

7. The words *guilt* and *forgiveness* do not occur in Paul's letters except when he is quoting Scripture or oral tradition; *repentance* is not used in any of Paul's theological arguments; and the word translated *forgiveness* is, in the Greek, actually related to *gracing* someone. Paul surely knew the pattern of sin-guilt-repentance-forgiveness within his tradition. The absence of this pattern in his own thought is, therefore, significant. Its absence is not due to ignorance of the pattern but to his choice not to include it.

8. See Rom 3:23.

9. Robin Scroggs, *Paul for a New Day* (Philadelphia: Fortress, 1977), 7.

10. That is, human existence apart from Christ.

11. Remember that theological terms are shorthand expressions for larger complexes of ideas about the relationship between God or ultimate reality and humanity.

12. The illustrations regarding children and parents are suited to the dynamic between God (as Creator) and humans (as created beings). Such analogies are always

limited and depend, to some degree, upon our own individual experience of family. Allow a certain flexibility in the analogy and be willing to assign to the "analogical parent" a more thoroughgoing positive aspect than you may be willing to ascribe to your literal parents. It may be helpful to discuss your view of the ideal parent.

13. See Rom 5:6, 10.

CHAPTER 6: SLAVERY AND DEATH

1. *Autonomy* means literally "self-rule." In the West, at least since the Enlightenment, individual autonomy has been seen as the goal of human maturity. Other cultures identify this goal differently. It is also the case that autonomy has traditionally been the goal for males in the West, while heteronomy (see below) has been the goal for females.

2. John K. Ryan, trans., *The Confessions of St. Augustine* (Garden City: Doubleday, 1960).

3. That is, you misperceived their commitment to you and to your joy as an effort to control you. See chapter 5.

4. See Rom 6:23, "For the wages of sin is death."

5. Scroggs, *Paul for a New Day*, 6.

6. Some would say that this is one of Paul's most absurd beliefs.

7. Literally, *heteronomy* means "other-rule." That is, in contrast to autonomy, we are heteronomous when we allow others (either individuals or institutions) to determine what we do and what we think. Our sense of self is drawn more from our relationship to others than it is from something internal to ourselves.

8. These are culturally inculcated values. The society of Japan, for instance, considers allegiance to the group rather than self more as the norm.

9. Heteronomy is especially concerned with the question of "staying in." While E. P. Sanders's distinction between how the law functions for "staying in" in distinction from "getting in" is a helpful critique of a common misunderstanding of Palestinian Judaism, that distinction obscures the more fundamental philosophical problems of heteronomy, authority, and the desire for security. See E. P. Sanders, *Paul, the Law, and the Jewish People* (Minneapolis: Fortress, 1983), 5–10 and passim.

CHAPTER 7: PAUL, AN APOSTLE OF CHRIST JESUS

1. You might also want to read Acts 9, the author of which (who wrote several decades after Paul's death) narrates a somewhat different version of God's revelation to Paul.

2. *Gospel* means "good news."

3. See Philippians 3.

4. That is, Paul shifted from an already established interpretation (Pharisaic) to what he understood to be a radically new (and thus not yet established) interpretation. See illustration 10.

5. Broadly defined, a mystical experience is one in which a person experiences union with the divine.

6. As stated in chapter 1, *apostle* means "one who is sent." The word refers to those of Jesus' followers who actively proclaimed the gospel (the good news) about Jesus' death and resurrection to others. In this context, *call* refers to the initial encounter between the human and God, who requests or demands some act on the part of the human.

7. We don't even have a full metaphorical narrative, much less a full phenomenological description.

8. We've already seen how Paul's use of the word *sin* (as an apocalyptic force of misperception) differs from another Jewish use of the word (as a violation of the commandment).

9. Keep in mind that a modern person's understanding of these words is very likely not Paul's understanding. We must unlearn in order to learn.

CHAPTER 8: JUSTIFIED BY GRACE

1. See Genesis 17 for the story of how circumcision came to be the "sign of the covenant" between God and Abraham.

2. See, e.g., the summary of the event that lay at the foundation of Israel's relation with YHWH—the exodus: "Israel saw the great work that the LORD did against the Egyptians. So the people feared the LORD and believed in the LORD and in his servant Moses" (Exod 14:31). For Israel, God's gracious act of salvation comes prior to faith, not as a result of faith. God always acts first.

3. It is this very element of surprise that constitutes the Aha! of revelation.

4. This is Paul's heresy in relation to later, normative, i.e., rabbinic, Judaism.

5. Of course, it may be just the opposite as well. We may measure our lives by how different we are from our parents. But whether or not we seek approval, the parents are still the defining term.

6. Measurement is, after all, only possible within a finite system.

7. The history of Israel attests amply to this fact. Abraham, Jacob, Israel in Egypt, David, the prophets—all were called by God without regard to their qualifications. One standard feature of call narratives is the human respondent's protest that he does not qualify for God's call. See, e.g., Exodus 3, Isaiah 6, Jeremiah 1.

CHAPTER 9: SPIRIT AND COMMUNITY

1. See the third definition of righteousness, page 29.

2. See the second definition of righteousness, page 26.

3. Ephesians was most likely written by a close disciple of Paul's sometime after Paul's death. This passage reflects a view of the law (i.e., that the law had been abolished) that was somewhat different from Paul's own view. But the passage states succinctly how Paul's teaching regarding justification apart from the law necessarily has an impact on the "dividing wall" between Jews and Gentiles.

4. See especially Paul's Letter to the Galatians and Romans 9–11.

5. To be human means to be a creature of God, to be a creature who is created in the image of God.

6. Look back to the beginning of chapter 6, where we first met Paul's apparently conflicted statement that the law, which seduced humanity into sin, is nonetheless "holy and just and righteous."

7. *Antinomian* means "against [*anti*] the law [*nomos*]."

8. Heteronomous action is against the law because it uses the law, rather than God's righteousness, to provide safety.

9. Though, by presuming that we are unlimited, we set higher standards for ourselves than our Creator does. And thus we are unable to measure up because we've misperceived our situation in the first place.

10. Aristotle, *Nicomachean Ethics* 2.3 (trans. T. Irwin; Indianapolis: Hackett Publishing Company, 1985), 46–51.

11. That is, Paul's view was not that individual humans should demonstrate a balance of autonomy and heteronomy. The community will demonstrate such balance, but individuals will, even in Christ, have proclivities toward either autonomy or heteronomy. In Christ, however, these proclivities become *charismata* rather than instruments of sin.

CHAPTER 10: FAITH AND HOPE

1. A creed is a brief statement of faith—an articulation of a group's primary life commitments.

2. This is, in fact, the importance of the phrase "and he was buried" in the 1 Corinthians creed. The burial was the proof that Jesus had really died.

3. This was the miracle of the resurrection. First-century people were not bound by a literalistic scientific mentality as we are today. Our scientifically (de)formed literalism (either in accepting or rejecting) too often allows us to evade confronting the major claim of the early believers in Christ: that God has inaugurated the new creation. In some ways, this is a much more startling claim than that God has simply resuscitated a dead body.

4. *Redeem* comes from the sphere of economics. When someone takes something to a pawn shop, for instance, and then returns to buy it back, this is called redeeming the item. The item again belongs to its original owner.

5. We could, indeed, define heteronomy as being something that arises out of a blind faith in relation to the law. One follows the law blindly, believing that in doing so one will be secure. But this very blindness is what makes heteronomy a trap.

Suggested Reading

Augustine. *Confessions.* Trans. John K. Ryan. Garden City: Doubleday, 1960.

Beker, J. Christiaan. *Paul's Apocalyptic Gospel: The Coming Triumph of God.* Philadelphia: Fortress, 1982.

Cousar, Charles B. *The Letters of Paul.* Nashville: Abingdon, 1996.

Furnish, Victor Paul. *Theology and Ethics in Paul.* Nashville: Abingdon, 1968.

Jaffee, Martin S. *Early Judaism.* Upper Saddle River, N.J.: Prentice-Hall, 1997.

Jewett, Robert. *Saint Paul at the Movies: The Apostle's Dialogue with American Culture.* Louisville: Westminster John Knox, 1993.

Käsemann, Ernst. *Perspectives on Paul.* Philadelphia: Fortress, 1971.

Keck, Leander E., and Victor Paul Furnish. *The Pauline Letters.* Nashville: Abingdon, 1984.

Malherbe, Abraham. *Paul and the Thessalonians.* Philadelphia: Fortress, 1987.

Meeks, Wayne. *The First Urban Christians: The Social World of the Apostle Paul.* New Haven: Yale University Press, 1983.

_____, ed. *The Writings of St. Paul.* New York: Norton, 1972.

Roetzel, Calvin J. *The Letters of Paul: Conversations in Context.* 4th ed. Louisville: Westminster John Knox, 1998.

Sanders, E. P. *Paul.* Oxford: Oxford University Press, 1991.

Scroggs, Robin. *Paul for a New Day.* Philadelphia: Fortress, 1977.

_____. *Christology in Paul and John.* Proclamation Commentaries. Philadelphia: Fortress, 1988.

Soards, Marion. *Paul: Apostle to the Gentiles.* Louisville: Westminster John Knox, 1993.

Stendahl, Krister. *Paul among Jews and Gentiles.* Philadelphia: Fortress, 1976.

Wright, N. T. *What Saint Paul Really Said: Was Paul of Tarsus the Real Founder of Christianity?* Grand Rapids: Eerdmans, 1997.

Glossary

Abraham

The "father of many nations" who received the original *covenant* from God. See Gen 12:1–3; 15; 17. Paul focuses on Abraham's faith. See especially Romans 4.

Adam

The first human. See Genesis 2–3. In early Jewish thought, as in Paul's thought, Adam was a symbol both for the original human created in goodness and for human sinfulness. See especially Romans 5.

age to come

In *apocalyptic eschatology,* the future age when God will rule.

apocalyptic (see *eschatology*)

apostle

"One who is sent," including not only the original disciples of the historical Jesus but also those missionaries of the early churches who were sent to preach the *gospel.*

autonomy

Literally, "self-rule," autonomy refers to the drive to determine one's own life. At its extreme, autonomy is equivalent to pride.

baptism

The rite of initiation that included immersion in water, practiced by the early churches. See Romans 6.

call

An encounter with God where God summons a human to perform a specific task or follow a life vocation. Paul was called to be the Apostle to the Gentiles. See Galatians 2.

charismata

Literally, "gifts." The gifts that the Spirit of God enables in humans. See 1 Corinthians 12 and Romans 12.

circumcision

The Jewish rite of initiation. Removal of the foreskin of Jewish boys eight days after their births. See Genesis 17.

conversion

Turning away from one religion or philosophy in order to adopt a new religion or philosophy.

covenant

An agreement (or contract) between two parties that is based upon a prior relationship and that enables the relationship to continue "forever." See Genesis 15 and 17 for the covenant that God made with Abraham. See Exodus 19–20 for the covenant that God made with Israel at Mount Sinai.

Christ

The revelation of God's *righteousness. Christ* is a translation into Greek of the Hebrew word for Messiah. Literally, it means "the anointed one." "Messiah" was a title for the anticipated future ruler of Israel. Paul and the early Christians applied the title to Jesus of Nazareth after his death and resurrection.

cross

A symbolic reference to the historic event of the crucifixion of Jesus of Nazareth by the Romans.

death

In Paul's thought, death is the primary symbol for impossibility, for the hopelessness and impotency of human life.

Diaspora

Jews who live outside Palestine are Diaspora Jews.

eschatology

Literally, "the study of last things," e.g., afterlife, heaven, hell, resurrection.

promise-fulfillment — The simplest type of eschatology: something is promised and then that promise is fulfilled. See illustration 1.

prophetic — When the promise is not fulfilled because of failure to remain committed to its fulfillment, *repentance* is needed in order to turn oneself around and renew one's commitment to the fulfillment. See illustration 2.

apocalyptic — When *repentance* fails to work, the failure is ascribed to the rule of evil powers who have enslaved the world.

The expectation emerges that God will intervene and defeat the powers, bringing this present history to an end and inaugurating a new age where God will rule. See illustration 3.

exaltation

A close synonym for *resurrection*. The early followers of Jesus believed that after Jesus' death, God exalted him to the position of lordship. The emphasis is on the spatial dimensions of God's revelation in *Christ*— both "in heaven and on earth."

faith

A commitment to live on the basis of *grace*, rather than on measurement or achievement.

flesh

Human drives and desires. In Greek, *sarx.* For Paul, *flesh* itself was not negative; rather, he cautioned against living "according to the flesh." Related to misperception.

gospel

Literally, "good news." Refers to the message of Paul (and other early believers) that God had acted redemptively in *Christ* Jesus.

grace

Literally, "gift." Paul proclaimed that *justification* comes as a free gift from God, apart from the *law*.

heteronomy

Literally, "other-rule," heteronomy refers to the drive to allow others to determine one's life. At its extreme, heteronomy is equivalent to slavish dependence.

hope

One's confidence that God, who has already acted in *Christ*, will bring full *shalom* to the entire cosmos.

justification

The act of making righteous or being made righteous. According to Paul, justification comes by *grace*, not by works of the *law*. Humans are graced with God's *righteous-*

ness, instead of achieving their own righteousness.

process of justification The means by which, as understood by Israel, the *covenant,* once broken, is renewed with God. See illustration 6.

law

Refers primarily to the *Torah,* the law that God gave Israel on Mount Sinai. See Exodus 19–20. In Jewish thought of Paul's day, the law was God's guidance to Israel, providing the means to *shalom.* Paul's own view of the law is complex. He continues to affirm the goodness of the law (see Romans 7) but emphasizes that God's *righteousness* comes to humans apart from the law. The law is no longer the determinative element in the relationship between God and humans.

monotheism

The belief that there is only one true God.

Moses

The leader of Israel who received the *law* from God. See Exodus 19–20,

mystical experience

An experience, usually ecstatic, of unity with the divine.

original sin

The idea, developed by Saint Augustine, that every human is infected with *sin* at conception.

Pharisee

The Pharisees were loosely associated scholars of the Jewish law, particularly concerned with maintaining the oral traditions that sought to guard the sanctity and obedience of this law.

process of justification (see *justification*)
promise-fulfillment (see *eschatology*)
prophetic (see *eschatology*)
rabbinic Judaism

A form of Judaism that had its roots in the 90 C.E. academy of rabbis who met at *Yavneh* to redefine Judaism after the destruction of the temple. This form of Judaism was determinative for all post-second-century Judaism. It produced the *Talmud* and emphasized the *law* as central to Jewish definition.

reconciliation

Bringing enemies together. Paul uses the term to refer to the mending of the relationship between humans and God and the bringing of Jews and Gentiles together.

redemption

Originally an economic term, meaning "buying back." In *Christ,* God redeemed the world from the *apocalyptic* powers who had enslaved it.

repentance

Literally, to "return" (Hebrew, *shub*). Repentance is the appropriate response when someone breaks a *covenant* but wants to see the covenant restored. Paul does not use this word as a key term in his theology.

resurrection

A term that refers to Israel's hope for the *age to come* when God will rule. As the defeat of death, resurrection is not simply a resuscitation of a corpse but declares the temporal dimensions of God's revelation in *Christ.*

righteousness

1. God's *shalom*-making activity.
2. God's *covenant* faithfulness.
3. God's repairing of the covenant when it has been violated. See *justification.*

saints

Paul's term for the group who believed in God's revelation in *Christ.*

sarx (see *flesh*)

Septuagint

The Greek translation of the Hebrew Scriptures.

shalom

Literally, "peace." Refers to the wholeness that God intends to bring to the cosmos.

sin

An *apocalyptic* force that controls humans, resulting in human impotency, misperception, and despair. Sin perverts human response to the *law* and leads to *death*.

slavery

Humans are enslaved by *sin* and thus unable to know *shalom*.

Spirit

The Spirit of God. Contrast with *flesh*. To live according to the Spirit means to understand life from the perspective of God.

Talmud

A large collection of oral *law* and commentary on that law, codified about the sixth century C.E. Authoritative for *rabbinic Judaism*.

Ten Commandments

A short summary of *Torah*. See Exodus 20.

Tetragrammaton

The four letters of God's name: YHWH. See Exod 3:14.

Torah

The Jewish *law*. Also refers to the five books of *Moses:* Genesis, Exodus, Leviticus, Numbers, and Deuteronomy.

universal citizenship

An emphasis of Greco-Roman philosophers who taught that the true human was a "citizen of the universe" rather than merely a citizen of a local people.

Yavneh (or Jamnia)

The city where rabbis met in the late first century to redefine Judaism after the fall of the temple.

YHWH

The *Tetragrammaton*. The holy name of God given to *Moses* in Exod 3:14.

Subject Index

Abraham, 14–15, 26, 42, 73–74, 91, 97–98, 100–101, 108, 138, 147, 151, 152
acceptance, 30, 96, 101, 115
achieve, 58, 76, 81, 104
Adam, 51, 52, 54, 60–61, 63, 80, 124, 127, 141
addiction, 57, 59, 74, 129–31
Adler, M., 143
adherence, 71, 77–78, 100, 108, 110
adolescence, 6, 62, 69, 71, 100
age to come, 123–25, 138, 151
alcoholism, 57–59, 115, 129–31
Alexander the Great, 49
alienation, 63, 70, 103, 116
analogy, xi, 3, 7, 42–43, 67, 100, 144, 145, 146
anthropology, 3
antinomian, 113
apocalyptic, 16–19, 21, 42, 54, 75, 88–89, 91–93, 123–28, 135, 140, 145, 146, 151, 152, 153, 154
apostle, xi, 1, 3, 5, 12, 15, 20, 42, 86, 88, 102, 104, 138, 143, 146, 151
approval, 100, 101
Aristotle, 1–2, 116–17, 119, 147
atonement, 92
Augustine, 69, 81, 146, 149
authority, 6, 68, 70–71, 75, 107, 127
autonomy, 65, 67, 69–72, 75, 77–78, 80–81, 103, 114, 116, 146, 151

baptism, 97, 111, 138, 151
Beker, J. C., 149

believe, xii, 3, 6–7, 18, 21, 61–62, 92, 97–98, 128, 135, 140. *See also* faith.
body, 3, 88, 97, 98, 110–11, 117–18, 123, 130, 133, 141
Borg, M., 143

call, 12, 26, 87–88, 103, 108, 138, 146, 147, 151
charismata, 114, 116, 119, 138, 151. *See also* gift.
Christ, 3–5, 7, 11–12, 14–15, 18, 20, 23, 41–42, 54, 77, 80, 85–88, 90–93, 95–96, 102–5, 107–8, 109–14, 116–18, 121–22, 124–25, 127–31, 134, 137–38, 141–42, 148, 152, 153. *See also* Jesus.
Christian, Christianity, 4–5, 11–12, 18, 20–21, 38, 56, 60, 102, 122, 127, 134, 144, 145, 152
church, 1, 2, 4–5, 12, 20, 26, 37, 87, 92, 137, 151
circumcision, 12, 97, 103, 110–11, 147, 151
commandment, 30, 56–57, 66–69, 73, 75, 91, 99–100, 111, 146; seize the commandment, 66, 72–73, 80
commitment, 5–6, 26–28, 37, 42, 68, 70, 80, 87, 111, 123, 129–31, 134, 138, 147, 152
community, xii, 12–13, 41–42, 49–50, 54, 79–80, 90–91, 93, 109–11, 114, 116–18, 134, 137
confession, 13, 56, 127–28, 130
contract, 27–29, 31, 35
conversion, 11–12, 48, 87, 138, 151
cosmos, 16–17, 19, 24–25, 35, 37–39, 41, 50, 80, 91–93, 121, 128, 131–32, 134, 138, 142, 144, 152, 153

Scripture Index